I'LL SHOW YOU

Derrick Rose
with Sam Smith

30 YEARS®
TRIUMPH
BOOKS

Library of Congress Cataloguing-in-Publication Data available upon request

This book is available in quantity at special discounts for your group or organization. For further information, contact:

Triumph Books LLC
814 North Franklin Street
Chicago, Illinois 60610
(312) 337-0747
www.triumphbooks.com

Printed in U.S.A.
ISBN: 978-1-62937-642-4
Design by Patricia Frey
Photos courtesy of Derrick Rose unless otherwise indicated

*I want to thank whoever is looking over
me and blessing me with my talent.*

*And I could never have gotten through what I did if it
wasn't for my family. I want to say thank you for raising
me with tough love and allowing me to be my quiet self.
I will forever be thankful and mindful of everything you
sacrificed to get me where I am in life. I love you all.*

"I'LL SHOW YOU" IS THE TITLE I wanted for this book. Because it represents me, my story, who I am.

Let's see what you can do. Not what you tell me you're gonna do—what you can do.

It shows both sides of my personality. I'm an introvert. I didn't understand for a long time what that meant. There's nothing bad or wrong with that. But it can make people think different about you. They think you think you're all that, or something.

That's not me; never been me.

But it's also having to do interviews when you're so young and no one tells you what to do or it's not something you're good at. Then people think of you in different ways.

Did you ever think back to when you were 17 and 18? And then you're 19 and 20 and in the NBA with all these reporters asking you things all the time? Ever think about what you'd say and how you would do that if you were a quiet person?

"I'll Show You" means "I lead by example." And that's pretty much how I did everything in my life. Watch me—don't wait for me to tell you. I've never been one to talk about it. It's also one of the reasons I never talk in basketball—none of that trash talking. It never bothered me. I kind of feed into it, anyway. "Alright, that's where we are at now? Just watch this now. I'm going to score this next bucket and we'll see if you look at me the same way." You gotta feel it. When I'm on the floor I'm totally different. What do they say in Chicago? They call it "not going," where you're just not backing down. I don't have to talk crazy on the floor. I can show them.

From growing up, too. It's just how I carry myself. You never know for sure why you are the way you are. But growing up where I did and seeing what I saw, I think that's one reason I like to be quiet.

Drugs were a big thing where I grew up on Chicago's South Side, in Englewood. I'm sure you've all heard about it. It's in the news all the time and this current president makes fun of it. It was home, a home to a lot of good people who care and are trying to make a better life, and stuff like that's unfair to the people there. They're trying to survive like people everywhere; they just don't get the same chance like people in other places. When you get out, you see the racism you didn't understand as a kid. People there are like people anywhere else. They want the same things.

But that cycle of violence, it's a dangerous place to grow up. I had friends die, heard gunshots, was scared in my house seeing people drive up with bats and sticks and ready to fight. I ran upstairs in my house. One of the reasons why I'm quiet, I think, is because looking at the drug trade, those loud guys were all the ones who went down. All the ones who were flashy and wanted to be seen, something seemed to happen to them. I never wanted to be that person. It was too many people in my neighborhood, they talked so much shit and I realized they always were the dumbest ones. I'm dead serious.

I'm seeing that as a kid. I'm thinking to myself, "If I ever get out of this situation, if I ever get a grip or something, I'm never gonna walk around like that, because it's too much attention." I could be quiet and seem dumb and nobody will know about me. Then I may hit you with a fun fact and that may blow your mind that day. You just don't know what I know. That's the way I wanted to come across.

That's what blows my mind. It would become, "Why should I give you that other side of me when you're shitting on me?" I show people that real side when I'm feeling warm enough to show it to you. It's the respect and vice versa.

I GOT A LOT OF ATTENTION from basketball, sure. But that's the part I cared about the least—the accolades. I think I realized early on it takes you to the wrong places. "I'll Show You" is like a little bit of attitude—no matter what I am, I'm determined to get where I'm going.

I was always told about how gifted I was when it came to basketball. And it's true. My speed, it was different. I could get places on the court, control the game without scoring. I never played a game against any of my brothers, because even when I was young they knew I was better than them even though they were so much older. I heard people compare me with Jason Kidd. But J. Kidd is not that athletic. He's gonna master his craft and what he does because he's not that athletic. He's bigger, learned how to shoot, great court vision. He's gonna use what he's got. With me, I feel like I had another side. And not just raw talent.

The speed. It kills, right? You could throw out everything else, but I had the speed to split double-teams. Like, go at double-teams numerous times in a possession, on consecutive possessions where I'm testing your endurance, your bigs. "How many times are you gonna be able to cut me off in that corner?"

Kevin Garnett was the best on defense. Really making me think the game. So I'm happy I came into the league when I did because the league now is totally different. But I was able to experience kind of what the old league had; I feel blessed to have experienced that, the tough play.

I played different in AAU than I did in high school. That's why my brother Reggie wanted me to have my own AAU team. It became sort of who I was on the court, the other Derrick. I played small forward in high school. I didn't have the ball in my hands. I wasn't the leading scorer on my teams. I didn't start scoring until I got to the league. When I played AAU, I wore No. 1 for the first time. That was like my alter ego, where I get to play the way I want to play and save my team.

It was at Peach Jam, the big Nike tournament. There were teams with Yao Ming, Tony Parker, everybody on the same team. I think that kind of helped me with the Bulls playing with mediocre players—mediocre scoring players. They were good players, but with the scoring I knew I couldn't let the game slip so far.

I know the game has changed even since I came into the league. Shooting is everything now. You gotta be able to shoot. But I've always felt I could adapt, like playing the three in high school, point guard in AAU, scoring when I needed to in the league. And I think you've seen when I got with Tom Thibodeau in Minnesota, with the pressure on Jimmy Butler and then after Jimmy was traded to the 76ers, how my three-point shooting was getting better. People forget it was getting better before the ACL. Then I got caught up in doing so many things to get back.

But the summer after I got to Minnesota, I'm shooting thousands of shots. So I'm not thinking about it. It's like the speed—you don't think, you just show people. I'm in the game. So shoot it. They'd say my shot didn't have the right arc. But did Kobe Bryant's? And all this when I'm back playing the three even, playing shooting guard, playing point. But I'm loving it. Remember, I'm 30, 31 years old. Not that kid anymore.

Sure, I've had doubts, but I feel I've shown that I'm mentally tough. I showed that even with what happened in New York and Cleveland, with leaving. I'm paying for that, but it was me. But I've been making history every time I'm on the court, and people can relate because everyone has struggles.

My critics could say I quit, but I never gave up. There's always been the love of the game, for my sons, my daughter. So me having my kids has played a huge role in pushing through these four, five surgeries, understanding my career and where I was, and where I am and where I will be.

A max player again? An All-Star? Sixth Man of the Year? I'm cool with that, too. I always feel anything is possible. Let my game speak for itself and let me be there as the vet to help my younger teammates grow and mature.

They always talk about my jump shot and what it was and wasn't. I always said I'm a hooper, and hoopers can do anything, I feel. It don't matter. Like, Marcus Smart is a hooper. Analytics, you would say no way you want him. But when you go out there and watch the game, you say, "Of course I want him on my team." Makes big shots, period. That's a guy I love playing with. That's what I mean when I say I'm a hooper. It don't matter if I miss 24 shots. I feel that 25th shot to win the game is going in. I feel like I'll make the right play at the right time.

I DON'T WORRY ABOUT THE INJURIES, haven't for a long time. People asked me about dunking in the playoffs when I came to Minnesota. I hadn't for a long time. It was just the fact of me being stubborn. I kept hearing people talk about dunking. "Dunk, dunk, dunk, dunk." Like, what? I know I'm way more than just a dunker. "You think that's basketball, huh?"

There's levels, and fans and media are just different. They're not always watching the whole game. They get bits and pieces on Snapchat and that can be their game. It's okay. But that's their takeaway from the game.

It's funny that I have this flashy game, you know? I heard someone say once it's a contradiction, that it's not my personality. I'm chill with my friends and family, but then on the basketball court, people see the game and it's the oohs and aahs. That's just my game, but that's also Chicago. Show them something. "Okay, I'll show you."

I know it might sound different, but I really believe my greatest gift is listening to people. I'm more observant—don't usually like being in the middle of things. You usually find that the loudest ones in the room are normally the dumbest, the most irritating ones. Nothing wrong with being an introvert. I didn't realize that until I got older. I used to be in social atmospheres and feel tired. Or I'd leave. I'd think, "Was it the workout or something?"

I didn't understand I was an introvert until I was 25 or 26. That's when I realized I need time to recharge my batteries. That's why when I'm with my family, it's always like,

"Oh, where's Pooh at? He's probably upstairs." That's the way I charge. You know what I mean? Charge myself.

I can talk to anyone; don't get me wrong. But afterward it's like, "Damn, I'm wore out." Like when I do the Adidas appearances when I go to China. I used to feel that in high school, too. It's an overload. You're doing interviews, promotional things. So sometimes people think you're arrogant or dumb or don't care. But it's just who I am. I did my talking with my game, doing what I had to do. People sometimes might feel like I'm not friendly or I'm not outgoing, but I can't help it; that's who I am. I'm used to it.

That's one of the things I used to worry about, too. "Damn, I gotta be more outgoing." Used to burn myself out doing that. Like with parties and events and stuff. Just visiting for a minute. Just trying to be there for like 30-45 minutes, running everywhere. But then after I leave it feels like I played an overtime game. People think you're famous, successful, got money, you can do everything. "What's your problem?" they'll think. "Too good for us?" It's never that.

That comes from my mom, watching her, being with her. I was her last kid—the good kid, the quiet kid. I didn't want to cause that trauma to my mom. My mom, Brenda, had me when she was 34. She's been everything to me. That's also why I always say everything happened for a reason. I remember when I was younger I'd have friends and their moms would be younger and they were going out and stuff, putting on hip clothes. My mom always had on more mature clothes. She wasn't going out.

I'm like, "Mom, where's your swagger?" You know? "Like, do something." But she was fit specifically for me. You know what I mean? Whereas I've seen her do things and dedicate so much to me. So I'm thinking, "Man, if I could do that—just a piece of what she did for her family—I'm gonna be good because she sacrificed everything for her family, for me and my brothers." She was the inspiration, the model. She was working a lot. She was paying all the bills in the house, always had a job.

I would isolate myself from friends and family a little bit, but not in the way where I'm totally gone. I wanted to show them that I could handle everything by myself. I get that from my mom. Straight independent, don't need nobody. I always wanted to be like her. Both her husbands she was with, it was like, "Heck with y'all. I don't need y'all. I can do my own thing with my four boys. I can take care of all of them."

"I'LL SHOW YOU," of course, was in Chicago basketball. I never really knew about Chicago basketball. All the older players, like Jamie Brandon and other names you'd hear when you were young—not Michael Jordan. I used to hear people compare me to them. That happens in Chicago all the time when you're growing up if you're a hooper. It's like, "Boy, you play just like Jamie Brandon."

I'm like, "Who?" They'd say he played for King. So alright, they're putting the expectations on you right away. You're playing under extreme pressure every night in high school. They do it in grammar school now. But with a lot of kids who get out and kind of make it, this makes you a tough player.

That was big for me with all the injuries when I got to the NBA. Not just the injuries and the rehab, but when the injuries came, things started to be different, people were different. People were just so wrapped up with me. It could be the smallest things. It might be, "I didn't like him in this interview," or "I didn't like what he said about that," and, "Oh yeah, by the way, ain't he injured, anyway?" You know what I mean?

Eventually I stopped trying to fight it. I know why you're mad. A good player plays. I'd be mad if I went to a Dodgers game and Clayton Kershaw isn't pitching. I'd be like, "Why am I at this game?" I get it. But I can't help the fact that whatever happened, happened. And it happened for a reason.

I'm a more enlightened person now. I felt like I used the time I had off to better myself as a person. That's what made me feel good about everything. So me even being in the league now and doing everything I'm doing, that's my history. That's me making history. I'm not going to be the last one who gets injured or the last star who gets injured the way I got injured. But what I can do is show you a way—be an example to the next person, whoever they are. I can show the next person, "You don't have to stop or go back, there's more for you." That's where I'm at.

My "I'll Show You" thing when I got to the league was like me saying, "I'm here, I can play with y'all." That was in that first playoffs against Boston with the Bulls. We were kind of a new team, young vets. Had a new coach with Vinny Del Negro. Ben Gordon was our scorer and then we got things going at the end after we picked up John Salmons, a cool dude. We always had good dudes on the Bulls teams—especially Joakim Noah, Luol Deng, and Kirk Hinrich.

I was being more the point guard. Ben scored, Salmons scored. We get into the playoffs and we're going to Boston, the champs. Kevin Garnett was injured, but Ray Allen, Paul Pierce, Rajon Rondo, Hall of Fame guys, were there.

Take that first game against Boston in the 2008 playoffs. I get 36 points and we win in overtime, gain home court, and it's a seven-game series. That really was the start for me. It was a crazy series with all the overtimes, big plays by everyone—great fun. It also was me finding out that not only can I play with y'all, I'm playing against some Hall of Famers. It felt like straight AAU. The team was just riding with me. It was just one of my moments in the bright light. It was, "I'm here. I can play on this level." I believed I could, but you always have to show it. Not only am I playing against all these greats, but I'm challenging you. I'm making you sweat. I'm making you argue. Going back to the bench, thinking about stuff. It's like, "Who is that guy?"

My vision was so clear then on what I wanted to do. Win MVP. Bam! Win a championship. That was next. Every year it seemed like we lost to LeBron James, but it kept getting clearer and then injury, injury, injury. Then it faded away.

At that point it was like, "Damn, what's next?" It was tough, but I always had to look forward. Start small, take some small steps. Then what kept me going was I'd have one idea where I tried to have something push me along. Come back, and this game, try not to miss any free throws. Because I'm going from shooting 25, 27 times in a game to 15 to nine to then DNPs. So it's like, "Alright, free throws, I ain't gonna miss no free throws this game." And then, "Alright, defense." Just start small and then try to pick myself back up. That's what I was doing, making it another game within the game, another challenge to me to see what I could do, how I could be better and help the team.

It taught me to play with a purpose. Every dribble with a purpose. I really got that from Kobe. Kobe taught me so much just watching him, hearing him talk. It's why I mention him a lot when I talk about the game. It's special, the way he set guys up. He didn't waste dribbles.

John Calipari was the same way for me. Before I got to Memphis, I always played with the ball and dribbled a lot and I remember Cal kept blowing the whistle one day in practice—kicked me out of practice, in fact. "Don't dribble so much," he'd say. My brothers played, so there was always a ball around the house. So you dribbled. Think of Kyrie Irving.

Kyrie is a dribbler. I could cross you over now. But my job is to get to this spot. I'm just trying to get to this spot. Kyrie is trying to make you fall on the way to get to this spot.

Cal was telling me I'm getting past guys with one move. So why keep coming back to embarrass the guy? I used to do that. I had to get past that. It's just when you're playing with the ball too much and you're trying to embarrass someone. It's a Chicago thing, New York thing, playing in a city. You could feel it's a good move. Just like when a writer writes a paragraph or a page or whatever your goal is. Like, "Damn, that's a good move, good paragraph." Sometimes you go overboard. I caught myself in a lot of situations where I tucked the ball. Just getting to the league, talking to Kobe. Kobe actually talked to us in high school one time, but just random. It was around the time he was thinking of coming to the Bulls. He came to Simeon. I remember him saying every dribble he's trying to set you up. To *show you.*

I ALWAYS HAD THE MENTALITY, the "I'll Show You," even with my friends. When I was going to the gym working out, I wasn't telling them that. I wanted them to say, "Oh, I see what he's doing. He's been in the gym." But when the injury happened, it was the total opposite, to where I distanced myself. I was trying to find out who I was as a man—only 23, 24 at the time. You know, trying to hold up to all my responsibilities, learn about business, learn about fatherhood. Figure out who I am in this world.

It was just a weird time. But it became, "If I get another opportunity, I know where it's gonna go. If I get the opportunity, I'm gonna be back like an All-Star, signed to a good deal, maybe a max deal." Not a doubt in my mind. That's one of the reasons I came back to the league and signed with Cleveland for like $2 million. I bet on myself every day. I always did. It's nothing to me. I still feel I'm that talent, to tell you the truth. It doesn't bother me people don't think so.

I think some people just wanna talk about my old contract, about how many dollars I got paid when I was injured. Like, man, I don't wanna hear about it. That's basically what Charles Barkley and them were saying on TNT, that I'm done.

"Let's please stop talking about him on this show." That's what Charles said. "He's done."

That's just how it is. Even with people who say they don't like me, if I was to see them and we're getting on an elevator, they would acknowledge me. "Hey D-Rose!" Like with autographs. The ones who hate me, they'll see me, not say nothing. But when they get to their best friends, they'll be like, "Hey, guess who I saw today? Bitch-ass D-Rose. He was getting on the elevator." You know what I mean? You're gonna slander me, but you're gonna acknowledge I was there.

Come on, I get it. It's all a part of it. It's the game. Can't let it overtake you. Something I try to avoid. I never want to be that type of person. That's the message I want to send to others, to kids, to everyone. You're gonna be who you're gonna be. Period.

I think that's what makes my story what it is. When people stumble on my story they'll peel back the layers and take it for what it is. I just want them to see two things—that I could improve my ass off and that I was a dawg.

I didn't worry about basketball even with all I went through—winning all through school, high school, college finals, the MVP, and it looked like we were gonna break through and then my ACL, more injuries, leaving, coming back, from the bottom to the top, to the bottom and coming back again. Mostly I worry about how I'm gonna live my life. How my family can do certain things. How I'm fitting into society and what's going on in the world. That's what I care about. They think I still only care about basketball, but what do you think is gonna happen when I get to play consistent games?

I'll show you.

That's why now I wanna tell you my story, because I feel it's bigger than just me.

I DID THINK I WAS GOING TO BE THE GREATEST. That was really my problem. I feel like I'm a student of the game. I knew exactly what was going on. Where I was at, what I wanted to achieve. Championships, more MVPs, Finals MVP. Everything you could think of as an athlete. Knowing that I made it, achieved it by working hard. Never had a problem working hard— two, three hours in the gym, workout after workout. This is all I have to do? That's a *job*? For all that money? This is easy.

Then you throw the accolades on top of that and it instills even more confidence. I'm thinking I'd be the greatest small ever because I felt the league never resolved my speed, never could figure it out. They couldn't stop me, couldn't handle the speed. Even now. I don't do some of the things I did when I was young—emotional, wild—but the speed is there. Like, you could throw everything else out there, but I had the speed to test you, to make plays. "Okay, how many times you gonna be able to cut me off?" Alright, yeah.

Until the injuries.

It was my fault, you know, the injuries, the ACL, the MCL. But I have no regrets. It really was the best thing that could have happened to me. I know, you think I'm crazy saying that. It was like the Cavs, when I left that season. Before I could come back, they made me see a psychiatrist because I know they thought there was something mentally wrong with me.

That's just the kind of stuff that happens to me. It's partly my fault because I don't say much. A lot of people think you're dumb when you're quiet, or think something's wrong with you. But like I said, I learned there's nothing wrong with being an introvert.

Of course, I wasn't thinking this way about my ACL the day it happened, the day I got injured. But I wasn't thinking right about a lot of things back then. It was just that all my injuries finally gave me time to enjoy everything I worked for. Yes, for real. Even if it wasn't always perfect.

It was all hoop back then for me. Almost every summer, I did too much. I enjoyed it, don't get me wrong. But when I was a lot younger, it was, "We play tomorrow? Okay, I ain't gonna go eat tonight." The dude I'm going against, I was thinking, "Is he going to that Jay-Z concert? Well, if he is, I'm going to bust his ass tomorrow." That's the way I thought. I was always so locked into the game.

I'm sleeping at night, staying in the crib, not playing around. You become a robot. Normal stuff like walking down the street, going to dinners, being able to go to concerts before games. A lot of shit I didn't think was the right thing to do because I was chasing greatness. I wasn't doing those things. I didn't do anything, even go out to eat. It was like, "You don't deserve to go out to eat. You didn't win anything yet."

I always looked at it that way. I was holding off on vacays because hopefully one day I'd win a championship. Then I could kick back. That was the whole thing, the whole mindset. Push, push, push. Gotta get there. "Great players wouldn't do that," I thought, "be out like that. Great players lock themselves in."

I should have gone on walks more. I should have gone out to eat more. I should have gone to brunches. I should have gone to concerts more. Of course, I went to eat certain times, but most of the time I was in the house. Because I felt like I was getting the advantage over someone by doing that, that it was all about the hooping. They weren't and I was. "Get that edge," that's what I was thinking.

When you look at it now, being older, who cares about accolades? Really, at the end of the day, what is an accolade? You know what I mean? Do you know who was MVP 12 years ago? Who cares?

But back then I knew I had it in me, that it was what I was supposed to do. The game just came too easy for me. I didn't even have to score to win games. I could control the game and then...wham!

BEFORE MY ACL, everybody thought the 2011 season was going to be the one for the Bulls. We had lost to Miami in the conference finals the year before. It was in five games, but we had swept them in the regular season and then won that first game at home in the playoffs. We lost in overtime in Game 4, had two rough games, then lost a close one in the last game in that series. It seemed a lot closer than 4–1. It seemed like we were about ready. You know, you lose and that taught you to win. You always heard that with the Bulls against the Pistons—they had to take their setbacks and then it was their time. That was us in 2011.

We always thought we were going to win a championship. We were sure of it. With Thibs, I always felt we had a chance. Even when we were down 3–1 to Miami in the 2010 playoffs, I thought we'd come back. That was the year when Omer Asik got hurt in Game 3. If he didn't get hurt, I feel that would have changed the series because we were so much bigger. We were confident, but there were times during each game where we didn't execute. There were turnovers that killed us against Miami because they play that aggressive style of play. Really, just things we felt we could take care of after that experience.

They were trapping me in the first quarter, trying to make me waste energy earlier, tire me out. Miami had a good strategy. But our whole thing with that team and Thibs was that we just didn't want it to be easy. We welcomed what they were doing. We had the big guys with Jo, Omer, Carlos Boozer,

Kurt Thomas. We don't care who you are—it's not gonna be an easy game. It's not gonna be a cakewalk game. It's gonna be a game where it's grinding and you're gonna be kind of beaten up. Every time someone goes through the lane, you hit them. Make sure LeBron goes to the hole, then you hit. Two people jump for the shot basically. Little things like that. We wouldn't run from that. Bring it!

They'd put LeBron on me and, being from Chicago, that's what you want. I was wishing he was guarding me the whole game so I could get him tired. I wasn't gonna pass the ball then. But I think they knew that, so that's why they had him just picking me up in the fourth quarter. We did all those things, took on what they threw at us, but they really were just great players making great plays. We'd feel like we overpowered them at some point during the game, but it always came down to little mistakes, turnovers, offensive rebounds, second-chance points, us maybe not being ready yet. That's what hurt most. But we also believed it would be our time. The Bulls went through it with the Pistons, the Pistons with the Celtics, a lot of teams had to lose and it really hurt before they could win.

The toughest loss was that Game 5 in the Eastern Conference Finals in the 2010 playoffs. Being up that many points in Game 5—like 10 or 12 with about three minutes left—we're thinking we had a grip on the game. It's about to be 3–2 and we'll be back in it and we know we can beat them in Miami and then we're going home for Game 7. That's how close we were even then. But then they made some great hustle plays and stayed with their routine and they ended up grinding out the game and winning the series.

It hurt more because we were supposed to be that team, the one to grind out the game. I just remember after it was done thinking, "Gotta get back in the gym." I think I took a week off and I was right back at it. It left a bitter taste in my mouth to end like that.

Every game we played against Miami under Thibs, it was intense, competitive, like a championship game. Great stuff. There were times where they blitzed me all game. From first quarter to fourth quarter. Not with LeBron because I was waiting for that, but blitz, blitz, blitz. It was just like chess. You know how the playoffs are—whoever makes the right adjustments, that's who's gonna win. They made the right adjustments. They tried to tire me out early and it did work. Turnovers, just overthinking. But I had to score for us to even stay in the game. So I was really overusing myself. They were trying to make me exhausted out there so I wouldn't have the energy to attack them on the offensive end. It was smart.

That's when me and BJ Armstrong, my longtime agent and a former champion in this league, started talking about how to approach games like that. We talked about how it's really okay for a team we're playing to be up big earlier in the game because I can still affect the outcome. Where if the game is close, I know what I could do. So the thought process was, "Alright, we're down 14, 16, it's gonna be tough, but I gotta try to get this to eight." You know, momentum—everyone makes a run in the NBA. Teams get tense, tight when that happens. That's what Miami did to us.

But we learned, and that's how I was looking at it coming into the next season. Don't get me wrong, all the teammates I had were great players. But there wasn't a star at that time, no Klay Thompson. I never really got into that. You're on my team, we're gonna play. But who wouldn't love playing with another great scorer? I wouldn't have minded a Klay-type guy, but looking back on it, I'm sure the Bulls wouldn't have, either. It just didn't happen. They would acknowledge that.

Jo wasn't that kind of player. He was more the grind-it-out player. Lu, Booz, they were great, but they weren't gonna take over a game offensively. But the first thing I thought every year while I was under Thibs was that we had a chance to win the championship or at least get there. I felt that way with who we had, with Thibs, the accountability, the expectation, just the structure, and everybody invested into the team from the vets to the rookies to the coaches. You know Thibs, he's fully invested. So everybody's invested. Front office was invested. It's just that we didn't get the job done yet. But we would. No way we weren't going to.

I really didn't feel like I was set back because of the lockout that summer going into the 2011 season. Some look back at that off-season and say that was the reason for my ACL injury, no regular training camp. No, I was still in my routine, working out at UCLA and I was going to Steve Jackson's house—the sneaker guy who has that Lakers court. I was going to his house to work out. But never playing pickup. That's something I learned from Kobe. I watch guys, but I always picked up a lot of stuff from Kobe. I don't know him that much, really. Did a sneaker commercial with him once—he kept me waiting like three, four hours. But it was all cool, though.

I think that it's dope that you don't see any of his workout videos. He was in the league 20 years. A great like he is, people around him see him play—you know he's great or he's gonna be great. But he's so secretive and so private that he doesn't even let videos of himself get out. That's what I like. Because what he's basically saying is, "I'll show you what I've been working on."

So during the game when he starts shooting threes, it's, "Shit, where did that come from?" And that's been my thing every year. Me sitting there and telling you, "I'm not gonna sell you on something. That's not me. I want you to look at the game."

"Oh shit! He changed his game."

When you play pickup, guys learn your tendencies. If I play against you a couple of times in just open gym, no coaches, I could basically learn what your tendencies are, how you dribble and all that. They call it analytics, but it's just what we see playing you. People know I'm a left-hand driver even though I'm right-handed. But it's still hard to guard sometimes because I don't give them an advance look.

WE HAD HOME COURT IN 2011 with the best record, and then in the 2012 playoffs we had home court again, the best record again, so, you know, it's time. We had our apprenticeship. I did have some injuries that season, but not big ones. I didn't play the last regular season game against Cleveland. But even with that and the shorter season, I felt I was ready, that we were ready.

The dream from the day I came to the Bulls was to win the championship for Chicago. When the Blackhawks won, I remember being motivated by them. I was dreaming about bringing that trophy home. Like, "Damn, they won two championships already? I gotta get one. Patrick Kane and them already got theirs." Seeing the parade, the celebrations, it motivated me. I wanted that for Chicago. This was going to be it. Almost 15 years after the Bulls' last one. It was time. I felt like I was ready. I was young. You never think much about anything. I was in shape. Just made that reckless move against the 76ers.

I felt we were just going to run through that first series, one vs. eight. They beat us one time early that season, but then we got them the last two times. We were leading by 20 that first playoff game and I felt good. They said I had 23 points and almost a triple-double, but I don't remember. I hardly ever remember what I scored. Just if we won. Because then you can't say anything to me. What you did, what you scored, you dunked, poster—I got the win. Smiling walking home. That's how I talk shit.

I just remember after I passed the ball when I came down. I remember it didn't tear all the way in my knee. I remember laying down by the 76ers bench. It got quiet, and when I stretched with my arms over my head it popped—it gave. My whole leg started trembling and I didn't have feeling in it or anything. I was able to walk. Got up and walked on it. That's why I was confused at first because I'm like, "I know something happened, but shit, I'm able to walk."

But they were like, "You can tear your ACL and walk." Walk with a torn ACL? No way!

"ACL." That's what you don't want to hear if you're a player. That's one of the things you keep hearing. The worst-case scenario. You hear it all over the league, "You don't want to tear your ACL." You hear the meniscus is a little bit easier to come back from. But the ACL, you have more time off.

I remember going in there praying that it wasn't the ACL. "Not no knee injury." Got to the hospital. Everybody's there. They put you in the MRI machine and I just remember crying and praying while I'm in there that it was nothing serious. And right when I came out, Dr. Brian Cole and the others were trying to hold it in, but they ended up telling me. My life changed right there.

I just remember my mom being there and she was telling me, "Alright, you're gonna get over this."

I'm crying, hysterical. Hard to accept. I'm saying, "I'm not gonna have my speed anymore."

She's like, "So what do you need it for?"

That was the type of talk she was trying to give me, but I wasn't trying to hear it. I'm thinking, "Let me get a grip on what's going on. And then I'll be able to talk to you. But right now I'm fucking traumatized." Like, my whole life, whole season, whole career, it's coming to a halt. And it's like, "Alright, what are you gonna do?" I had to ask myself that, because I had the chance of walking away. I had way more money than I needed by then. I had the chance of walking away and being totally fine with that.

But my mom was like, "This crying that you're doing, I ain't trying to hear that. Figure it out."

It just got real. When I was younger, everything that I dreamed for I got in some type of way. It wasn't a perfect path to get to where I got, but somehow I got there. Even picking the schools. I thought I was going to North Carolina. I ended up going to a small school, Memphis, and it still worked itself out. So when this happened it was like, "I have to restart everything." That's what I was thinking at the time. Not thinking I could use that time to sharpen myself or elevate myself, and just raise my vibration. I wasn't thinking like that. I was thinking just basketball. And I think that's why it changed me, because when I started thinking that way, I would isolate myself, and I'd think I can do everything myself.

I know some people said I shouldn't have been playing late in that Philadelphia game, that we were winning by a lot, I'm playing too much after being out here and there. Hey, I was the one who made that reckless move. I was going across the middle and I made the jump stop and I was passing the ball to the corner. There was no point making the jump stop. I could have hit him or brought the ball back. Collapse and go corner. I was too wild.

I heard that people said Thibs played me too much. I can't blame it on Thibs. He didn't control that. He didn't make me do that. I made that decision to still be in the game. Shit happens, that's how I looked at it.

It's all about how you come out of it. And how you learn from it, from the experience. I learned from it. I think I'm a better player now, really. I didn't know how to manage a game then. I feel like I know how to manage a game now, work better with teammates. I'm a totally different player, a different person. The thing I was missing after Cleveland and going to Minnesota was opportunity.

Thibs, we never talked about it, the injury. How could I blame that on him? I did the jump stop, I did the moves. I didn't have to do that. That's what I mean about being reckless. Why the fuck did I do that move? It's late in the game, we were up. Why? That's what I'm saying. Just doing some crazy, unnecessary shit, reckless, running around, you see what happened.

At first I was blaming myself. But I got to thinking and I began to eventually realize the reason for maybe why I'm here, the culture of people struggling, and the importance of being a symbol. Everybody's struggling. Things that go wrong. Everyone has problems. It's about how you react and come out of it. That's why I feel people can relate to me. No reason I shouldn't struggle, too. Before then I was living in a fairy tale or something like that. When that injury happened, I remember my mind clicking and thinking about the future, like, "Damn, what am I gonna do? How am I gonna get through this with this only my third year?" Thibs is kind of just like I am. He don't let nobody in until he trusts you. He showed me he trusted me. We had a close relationship. Still do. But that was the change. It was because it just made everything real.

That's where karma comes in for me. That's maybe what you'd say is my religion, what I believe in—my mom, too. She taught me that. She never yelled. Her thing is never giving up, no matter how hard it's going. She'd say some stuff she went through and try to get me to relate to it and try to get me to see it from her point of view. Hear her perspective on it. That's why I talk about karma.

My mom is in her sixties. She had two knee replacements and she never played sports. People laugh at me because of my injuries, but then I see my mom go through that and I'm like, "Y'all gonna go through that, too." That's how I feel. Everybody who laughed at me about my injuries, you all got your own thing. There's a timer on it. Are you gonna manage it right? I know God prepped me to be able to learn about my body—how to lose weight, what my body composition is. I know now about all that. Are you prepped for it, for what's coming for you? That's what I wanna ask them.

My mom had two knee replacements off just living. That's something I could relate to, sort of. She never really watched basketball. She only watched it because of the kids. We don't talk about hoops and sports like that because that's not her world. So we had something in common with our injuries. I'll say my legs hurt and she'll crack a joke to me. We laugh about it, our knee injuries.

I feel like you get what you put out; that's what I mean about karma. The energy you put out is the energy you receive. My mom talked to me about that. She always believed in it. I've never seen her mistreat anyone. If she cursed someone out, I felt like they deserved it. But she'd mostly bite her tongue. I treat people like I would want to be treated. That's from Mom. She always emphasized that. I always gave because Mom, she gives. We love seeing people happy. It could be small things, we just wanna be there. It's biblical, also. I believe in energy. You get what you give.

LOOK, I DIDN'T GET HURT IN A CLUB. I didn't get hurt in a car acci-dent, riding a motorcycle, snowboard. I got hurt at work! But I think it kind of matured me. Slowed me down, too. All these injuries. It happened to slow me down and give me some time to really enjoy living. I felt like I didn't enjoy my younger years the way that I should have.

I don't have a religion I live and die for. But some of them, I love their principles. My faith is really that I believe in a higher power. I believe in treating others right. I believe in the 10 Commandments. I believe in karma. I believe in good vibrations. I believe in the spiritual life. I believe in all that—I take a little bit from almost every religion.

Really, all religions are about patience. Just how you're gonna have patience in certain instances. You're gonna have struggles in your life. How are you gonna deal with it? Like with the media in Chicago after the ACL. I was mad the way I was being treated, but I handled it all wrong. I handled that situation with a hood-type mentality where I was fighting against it instead of just playing the game. I didn't grow. In interviews it was, "No!" I wasn't elaborating on my answers.

"Why should I?" That's what I was thinking. "Why should I elaborate on my answers when you don't deserve it?" I'd *show* them. "Why should I give you any good side of me? Period." And that was the wrong reaction because that meant they won. That's what you realize and learn—it was another thing I learned from all this. That's just not me. Maybe a little like LeBron when he did his TV show to tell everyone he was going to Miami. You react, but then you look back and realize that's not you. I feel at the time it stunted my growth. It sounds crazy, but that's another reason why all this was good for me, really saved my life, saved my career.

I was never as happy as I am now.

I never really miss being that guy I was before the ACL. I know I'm not him and never can be again, which is fine with me. Because that guy comes with not knowing who he really is. I feel like if I would have stayed on that path, I would have ended up being someone like Bobby Fischer, where I would have isolated myself, maybe for good. Because I'd be obsessed with the greatness. I've always been obsessed with that. I love hearing stories—or just looking up people and reading their stories—about how far people push themselves and how far they made it. It's something I can relate to, what people push themselves to. Like Bruce Lee—I've read tons about how he pushed beyond the limits.

I found out through all this who I really am. It made me learn who I am as a man. It made me more curious to see what else is out there. Try to learn as much as I can. Self-educate myself. I love to read history, the amazing things African American people did that no one realizes, things they were inventing, discovering, overcoming. I've always been fascinated with history. At the time I didn't know the word for it, but I remember saying they "just kept going." As a kid, I didn't know the word was "perseverance." They kept going. They didn't quit.

Like the way I was growing up in Chicago. That's one of the reasons why Chicago is also my story. As a kid, you are brought up to not back down. Hit 'em back. Hit 'em back right now. You don't let nobody hit you again. But I wasn't that aggressive type of dude. That wasn't my character. I always gave people respect because I wanted it back. I was losing who I was with who I was becoming. The injury was like a wake-up call for me.

What I also learned is that it's just a sport, just a game, just something to keep you entertained. And it so happened that I was fit for that system. Like being a pawn. And, of course, it's only momentary even though you aren't thinking like that. You find that out. I felt like if I didn't get injured they were gonna ride it out on me, too. You see what they're doing with Steph Curry right now? I mean, a couple years ago, Steph is everything. Then it's Kevin Durant to the team. You would've thought they were handing the league over to Steph when he won the MVPs. But what happened? Injuries. It's the circus. It's the next young act.

Perseverance. That's what made Kobe who he is. That's why I admired him so much. You know you're not gonna be number one in the league forever, but to be 14 years in and still be number six or whatever he still was? Not holding guys off, but playing through adversity. All this going on in the league, Kobe played through everybody's greatest—LeBron, Tracy McGrady, Garnett. And he went through a lot of stuff off the court. Kept going. You can just tell he had the discipline to be that good.

When BJ talked to me about how much revenue I was bringing into the city my rookie year, I started to get it. We're going over stuff about the Boston playoff series in my rookie year. I never thought anything about that. I was only thinking it was artists who had that impact, musicians who come in for a concert or something. I wasn't thinking of myself as one of those people. They were the people I went to see. This was about the team. You get what I'm saying? It's about everyone.

But I'm realizing Kobe comes to town—you think fans come to see Kwame Brown or Kobe? You start looking around the stadium, start seeing what jerseys they have on. It all opened my eyes to see what was going on. You're a kid brought up like I was, just hoopin', big games, trips out of the city, but just basketball. You want to be one of them guys, but you don't think it's you.

It all began to make me more aware. It was way more than a game. I'm happy I got to experience that when I was younger, but then just as glad it ended. I would have been a screwed-up individual. I wouldn't have cared about people's feelings. I would have blamed everything on them. I would have just said, "You're a distraction, you're hurting me." All me, me, me. When you think about greats—Bruce Lee, Bobby Fischer—they got caught up.

Same with me back then. How much I stayed in the gym. That was what I could be confident about. I don't brag or boast, celebrate basketball like that. None of that. But as far as my work ethic and how much I put into it, nobody can tell me. The more successful I would have been, the hungrier I'd get. I would have wanted more.

So I don't regret anything that happened. Really don't. It's kind of cool looking back at it because the player that I am about to become, people are gonna see, "Damn, he totally changed his game." And even if my story doesn't reach a lot of people, the people that do stumble on my story when I'm gone or whatever, I hope they'll be able to relate with how hard I worked and what is important.

I think about what I call the hoop matrix. I was caught in it. When I was in that matrix, that's why I would say a statement like, "Why can't I be MVP of this league?" It was my second year and you had to be saying, "What the hell is he talking about?" Then I went and did it. It all fell into place because I played well enough and everything was working around me.

The media, the hype, all that, they go with whoever is winning. Now I really was all in. Then when I tore my ACL, I asked my mom, "Why? I just don't get it. Why, why, why?"

And now, being a little older and looking back at it and seeing how far I came from it, seeing how much I grew, now I do get it. I've really got a chance to change these kids' mindsets. Consider the area I'm from—South Side Chicago, Englewood. At the time one of my goals was to be a billionaire. I really was saying that to people. But I've changed. Now I wanna do something where I can someday start a foundation and have people work in the foundation and I'll be there for the foundation. It's still basketball for me now, but when it's time, I want it to be me there all the time. I want to be fully invested in whatever I do.

A lot of the kids out here where I'm from, they don't get that much love. It's a lot of stuff that plays out in kids' lives.

I want these kids to know that we need every one of them. We love them. I want these kids to stop thinking selfishly because the way they're thinking, it's like a video game, like they are in a game that don't love them back. And at the end of the day, who gets hurt is your family.

Kids need to learn—just be patient. Everybody wants it now. That's why I'm trying to stay away from Instagram. Social media makes you impatient.

I was 20 thrust into this world. Didn't know anything about my finances. Didn't know about trusts or wills, options, equities in bonds, media. I didn't know any of that. How are you supposed to? Thrust into it—an introvert, don't know shit about money. Don't know nothing about the league. Just want to hoop. Got a pure love of basketball. Good, bad, keep it moving. I'm having so much success.

But I didn't enjoy it. The MVP? Off to the side. Didn't cherish it. I don't remember a night when I went to eat with my family. None of that. Rookie of the Year? I was supposed to get that. "Okay, got the MVP. Let's see if I can get another one." It was too fast—which I wanted, but it wasn't enjoyable like I thought it would be. I was just putting everything to the side because I felt like, "I've got 15 more years of this." So just keep racking these up. I was locked in, but I was turning into this narcissistic person, trapped, stuck in that matrix.

There's only a few who are able to do both, the Michael Jordans, the Allen Iversons, able to party the same way that they played. That candle is gonna burn out on one end. I saw a lot of people burn out that way. I was trying to lock in and it was making me crazy. The ACL was the beginning of the end of all that.

I LIVED IN A CRACK HOUSE GROWING UP. The little bungalow house on Paulina, 7305. That's part of why I act the way I act sometimes. I remember taking crack pipes to my grandmother and asking her, "What's this?" She would grab it from me quick. I'm thinking I did something wrong. I thought it was a pipe and it was still burning, so I'm taking it to her thinking, "Get it before it explodes."

In the house, they were stealing things from me. They stole my ring, my baby ring. It had a P on it for "Pooh." They stole my *Home Alone* walkie-talkie thing to record the voices and all that. Stole it. I'm looking for it for like two years as a kid. Two years, imagine that. Thought I put it somewhere. They—uncles—were selling my toys, yo-yos, and Giga Pets.

There were maybe 10, 11 people living there. Mom's brothers, one of their wives, their cousins, my cousins, brothers, grandmother. The house was a four-bedroom house, but we were tucked into five or six little spaces all over. Pretty much anywhere you go upstairs, it would turn into a bedroom. Someone can go in there, sleep on the couch or something. The little walkways upstairs, that'd be a room. A little closet, but you could kind of fit, that'd be a room.

I was sleeping in the same bed with my mom before high school. There wasn't enough space. And, yeah, I was just more comfortable around my mom. By that time my brothers were already older. They were already moving around the neighborhood. You know how it is, they're not gonna have their little brother following them around. So most of the time I was by myself.

It was a crazy household, and I wonder sometimes if I have post-traumatic stress disorder, PTSD. Things were happening all the time. Like my cousin Keondra, she was always getting into fights. Usually winning. She was the tough one. She had the good sneakers, the new Jordans, all the time. When I was little, I used to take them to wear sometimes if there was a big game, because she had the ones with the tread. So I'd squeeze into them.

She used to get into fights in the neighborhood, so there were numerous occasions where I was playing out in the street or playing on the block and you see like four cars pull up in front of your crib and people jumping out with bats and guns. So as a kid, I could be anywhere in the house and I hear someone, like my cousins playing upstairs, wrestling, I hear them fall or bump when they're wrestling. But because of some of those fights outside, I used to think it was somebody coming in to get my cousin. So I'd run upstairs every time and hide. Thinking that somebody's breaking in. My heart's beating fast as shit. I'm thinking, "Damn, they're coming back."

She's in Chicago now. Doing good. But I also remember one of my friends with this older guy, they're in a car and the older guy says he's got to do a hit. But he ends up killing my friend, and he shot my other friend in the neck, but my friend got away because he pretended to be dead. Gang stuff. Stuff you just had to grow up with because it was around you in my neighborhood. You're not a part of it, but it's all around. You can try to stay away, but how do you really get away?

I know people are going to say it's because of the people there, the African Americans doing all this killing, that they don't care about anything. But that's the quiet racism nobody talks about, the racism they started, the racism that leads to all this. It's 2019 and you would think that as people, we would grow. Especially since it's been so long since slavery has been around.

Everyone likes to act like we're progressing in America, we're great. How can that be great? How can you be great when you can't confront your truth? The truth is you mistreat people. The truth is you tell people if you work hard and get a diploma you're gonna be gifted this opportunity of a lifetime, but a lot of people don't get the opportunity no matter what. They don't get the chance to even put a foot in that door.

People don't understand that living where I lived, there are a bunch of traps that you can get caught up in. This place traps a lot of people. People are locked up—more people are locked up than in slavery.

You look at the schools. Where do they close the schools? All over the South Side. And then they give money to help private schools for people who already have money. Look at the books we have, the labs, the prep for exams. It's not like other places in Chicago. And then they say people don't want to work, they just want free money. Fuck that. My mom worked two, three jobs, worked all the time. I'd ditch school sometimes, because she'd leave before me. But she was always calling to make sure I went. She'd get home after basketball practice, working all kinds of jobs, secretary, everything you could think of, but there still wasn't enough money because of how little these jobs paid. But she was always trying to work.

Look at all the stuff the Daleys did when they ran Chicago. You think there's no reason why the Dan Ryan Expressway was built where it was? They cut off the South Side neighborhoods to protect the Bridgeport area and the Daleys. The police were all over there protecting those streets in Bridgeport. Then the buildings come up—public housing, they called it—and it was like prison, high-rise buildings for people to live in like jails.

Don't tell me about Chicago and it's gangs with all the drugs. What was Chicago known for? Al Capone and Italian gangsters, right? Shooting up everything, what all the movies were about. You read about that 1893 World's Fair? All those women going missing. Nobody talks about that and they try to act like Chicago got crazy all of a sudden. They try to act like it's just blacks acting crazy. They try to act like it's these crazy negroes. Hey, Mayor Daley's family was doing the bootlegging. They had gangs back in the day going to neighborhoods beating up black guys. We're the problem?

It is a crisis now, but don't try to act like this suddenly just got here. Even in Chicago, how much opportunity do you have if you are African American? Chicago is low-key segregated. Here's what I mean. You can have money in Chicago, but then try to get a building or get property in certain places if you're African American. I've been turned down trying to buy property downtown. I tried to get a shop for my girl at the time to have a salon near Michigan Avenue. They turned me away. You know, I've got capital. They thought it was gonna be an "urban" crowd. You know what I mean? Coming down to *their* Michigan Avenue.

So not only are there not so many shops and companies in our neighborhood, and so not enough jobs, but then when you try to open something, they tell you no. And when they tell you no, somehow it's our fault?

How are we supposed to grow as a community?

So people end up selling drugs. Nothing big, my brothers did that. It's just for the family to live. This is no drug gang.

And how come with our drugs, we go to jail? Isn't alcohol a drug? Tobacco? But too many white businesses make money on that, so that's okay. So you think more people are getting killed driving with drugs or driving drunk? But it's the African American community that's the problem? That's why I wore the "I Can't Breathe" T-shirt after Eric Garner was killed in New York.

I know these kids and I know they really want to change. They want to have a chance at the same things everyone else does. That's why I try to keep asking if there really is enough opportunity where I'm from. Because I have money there and I'm *still* having a hard time finding someone who's gonna help my people prosper. It seems like we're in a system where you get cut off every angle that you go.

First off, to even get the job, are you educated? Think about school. Why is it costing so much money to go to college? What kind of country is this when we're not letting kids get educated because of where they're from? Health care, too. People going broke just because they got sick. That's fair? Isn't this the kind of stuff the country is supposed to be doing so you have better and smarter and healthier people? That's good for everyone, good for the country. The goal is for every generation to get smarter. So why charge somebody for that?

If the goal is to make sure that humanity and society are progressing, we need to pay for that, if you really care. We got enough billionaires in New York alone to take care of that.

It's crazy. Why is there a price on education and health? It's not something you think about when you're a kid because you just don't know. I've been really lucky to have basketball and everything me and my family got from it, but when you're older and get out there and start to look back, you cry for the kids.

Look, most of us don't even got our dads in the crib. So there goes the household basically for a lot of kids. I was lucky because my mom is so strong and I had my brothers and people close to us. But it affects a lot of kids. You feel hopeless.

That's what I'm trying to do now. Lead by example. It's kind of hard even to talk about it because, like I say, you would have to bring up everything that's part of the system. I know those kids want to do well. I'm around them. I know a lot of them. But a lot of the time they just don't have a chance. Don't got the resources. There's none of that. So it's survival mode 24/7. Where it's like, "What's next? What's going on? Alright, I can't go over there to that block."

There's millions of kids out there who don't have that same opportunity. That's why I wished I had the billion dollars I used to talk about. Because I'd know I really have a chance to affect a lot of things that are going on in society. But I will someday. I will be there again.

One thing I can do now is, I find out about buildings in Englewood when they come on the market. I haven't bought many yet because right now basketball still is my number one. I feel like you can't love two things at once. So I've got to concentrate on this. But I've done stuff to try to help, always quiet, which is just how I do things.

I worked with Joakim Noah and his foundation and Father Michael Pfleger and the anti-violence campaign. Fixed the rims and the court at my old park, Murray Park, right around the corner from our place on Paulina. I was there all the time, shoveling off the snow to play back then. Did that so the kids could have the court to play on. Gave that million dollars to the After School Matters program.

Not many can break out with basketball like I did, so I'm so proud of my Rose Scholars scholarship program. Alberto Ortiz from Tennessee received $10,000 in November 2018 for his education at Middle Tennessee State. Madison Carmouche-Soward from Alabama earned a $20,000 scholarship. Gabriel Lee from Phoenix was the grand prize recipient from Rose Scholars for up to $200,000 for his kinesiology work at Michigan State.

I'm looking forward to their futures. I'm so grateful I can do these things for people. It's really what I'm about. It's the kids, and if you're trying to add to society that's where I feel you. I had this NBA destiny from when I was young, but that's so rare. I was lucky and I had a path almost forced on me, though I wasn't complaining. But you want to make a mark in the right places, do something, and it has to be with education. I can be more hands-on after basketball and it gives my kids something to look at and be proud of.

Growing up the way I did with all the cousins and kids in the family, the house, the neighborhood, you want to help the kids. I love the scholarships because you are not only helping someone, you are helping the community, making it a better place for everyone, and who knows what contributions to the community these kids will come back and make? It's all about looking out for the youth.

I pay for funerals, stuff you don't talk about. I try to help quietly. I understand what you're going through. I know how much a funeral costs. I've been there. Lots of times. Where you try to bury somebody or someone you know is trying to and you don't have enough money. You're trying to scrape up money just to bury your loved one in a respectful way. How bad is that?

I've been there. I was the youngest one in the crib, so I was always around older people hearing the conversations. Maybe I was around conversations I shouldn't have been around. But in my neighborhood you heard about death a lot, and what to do, and it's sad. And then people don't even have money to do a proper respect? Somebody's getting killed right now and they have to figure out where they're gonna get the money from? Come on!

I DON'T LIVE IN THAT AREA ANYMORE, of course, but you've gotta know what's going on in that area. So I have people who live there that I communicate with. They tell me what's going on. I go back sometimes and ride through the area, seeing how I can buy properties and change the neighborhood. That's got to be what I'll be doing. I know now how to invest my money. I've got a great team, financial people, my agents, Arn Tellem before, and BJ Armstrong. Arn and BJ, I owe them everything. Looking back, the way they were looking out for me on everything, man, it means something. They made sure I didn't miss out on anything. For me to be in that position, they could have easily taken advantage of me. They didn't.

That's why I feel my story is for the ones who understand that struggle. You can relate to it. Even now people don't know about me like that. But I feel like they can feel what I've been through. I don't entertain on social media. No type of Instagram posts to draw fans into me like everyone else. But I feel they can feel something about me. I think it comes from being authentic, no bullshit, which a lot of times the media made into something for no reason. It's just being myself.

Like the "I Can't Breathe" T-shirt I mentioned. I'm from that same kind of neighborhood where that man got killed. That looks like every storefront in my neighborhood. I easily could have seen that, been there. And what could I have done with the police? Like, "Whoa, whoa, you got him in a chokehold! You about to kill him!"

I saw it so I talked to my best friend, Randall. I told him to put the words on a plain shirt. It was like a plea to stop. That was December 2014, Bulls vs. Warriors. And when I put it on and walked out there, I knew that it was gonna be something, because all my teammates, they were just shook. It wasn't about me, but you could tell they were thinking something different.

Would people be upset? Because I wasn't someone who talked much, wasn't someone always speaking up, I think that made it louder. But that's what I mean. Stuff like that. Something simple. Something I cared about. And it's helping others. That's how I wanted to express it.

The craziest thing is, I never experienced any encounters with the police like that. I'm light-skinned, which matters in my neighborhood. If you're light-skinned, they think you're soft. I never fought in my neighborhood. I only fought with my friends. I just carry myself different. I had to walk around like that, like I was tough, like I could fight. "As long as you don't try me, I'm not gonna try you."

I did get locked up in high school once, but it was for shooting dice. And really because I was light-skinned. No bullshit. The cop picked me because I was the innocent-looking kid. It stayed on my record until I was 17 or 18. If you don't have any violations after that they erase it. I was 15. I was in the back of the school, 20 or 30 kids out there shooting dice. But I'm on the court playing basketball. Somehow the officer snuck over there. The people who were shooting dice acted like they were involved in a basketball game. Starting to yell out, "I got next!" Then just walking around so the cop don't get 'em.

I'm on the court dribbling the ball. He comes up to me, out of about 30 kids, and he picks me. Why? He saw some type of innocence, I think. He knows all the other kids are gonna run and I don't wanna have a problem. You get shot running away. We'd seen that.

So they locked me up. I was in there for like six hours. My mom had to leave work. I thought she was gonna be more mad about having to leave work than picking me up from jail for getting arrested for playing dice, but she was cool. It had to come from my older brothers being in trouble. She knew this wasn't that serious compared to what they were doing.

My brothers got in some trouble, but mostly minor things. I think everybody except me and my oldest brother sold drugs when they were younger. They weren't kingpins or anything like that, where the reputation is, "Don't touch him." They weren't a distraction to the neighborhood. They didn't cause any ruckus. None of that. But you just knew if you messed with one of us, we were not gonna back down. It's not like we were coming to intimidate anybody. I just carried myself in a different way. The vibe is different. I'm not coming in with an ego. I'm not walking around telling you what to do or how to be, that was never me. When I was around people, it was more like, just let me be.

My brothers went to Hubbard High. They all played ball. Wayne ended up going to Amherst College for a little bit. Reggie went to a juco and then to Idaho U. Allan, he was supposed to go to Robert Morris in Pennsylvania to play ball. But Allan didn't go. I remember my brother Reggie pulls up on me in his car one day and he's like, "Where's your brother at?" He pulls off fast, so I knew something was up.

I went back home and by that time Reggie was beating up Allan because he said he wasn't going to college. So I'm seeing this and thinking, "He's doing that because he said he ain't going to college?" Well, I'm going to college after I see him whoop Allan like that.

Allan had a scholarship and everything, was the best player of the other brothers, but he got caught up in the hood. He became a big example for me, though, of what not to do. I saw how it changed my big bro. Not doing the drugs, but selling. Not in a gang, but just trying to make some money to survive, help the family. That's mostly what all those drug sales were about. They won't let you go downtown where you can open a business to give people jobs. You see stores closing in our areas, like those Target stores closing at the end of 2018. Then they open them in better neighborhoods. There go more jobs. I never sold drugs, never was into that. Saw my brother go through all that and I told myself I'd never go that route.

Allan is one of the biggest assholes I know. Aggravates everybody. He used to push me around when I was younger. He used to do it in a crazy way. I usually did pretty good at school. I only got one F in all of high school. But I got a D on my report card once; Allan would say, "They put D for dummy." Little shit like that. But he was smart, so I couldn't say shit back. One night he was bagging out these drugs and I was in the room with him. He never gave me a compliment. That's how I knew this was different.

He was like, "Don't ever do this shit what I do." I was just in his room chillin', just to be around. Then he says it again, "Don't ever do this shit."

I was like, "You don't gotta worry about that."

"Shorty," he said, "you cold."

That means you're really good—he meant really good at hoopin'. To hear him say that, I was like, "Damn, he knows I can hoop." My mom didn't. Nobody really knew I hooped like that when I was in grade school. But from word of mouth, people were telling him, "Yo, your little brother was up there."

He was the first to really know I could play, and I felt like I could play a little bit, too, so he warned me. He wanted to make sure I didn't pick his way.

In that sort of way, the neighborhood also takes care of its own. I saw it a lot. I think a lot of people didn't pick on me because it was like, "What's the point of picking on him? You don't get any points for picking on Derrick. He's quiet. He stays in his own lane. And he can hoop his ass off."

In my neighborhood, it kind of got to the point where everybody knew I was gonna make it. Imagine that as a kid. I'm seeing a crackhead every day, danger every day, but nobody in my neighborhood really tried to harm me or touch me because everybody knew I had a dream. I was getting through, getting out. It wasn't ever said to me, it was more like it was understood—just a weird feeling.

I'll tell you a story. I never sold drugs, but I gambled. Dice and basketball. Those were my games. The guy that I'm telling you about, Deion, he's dead now. But when I was younger I kind of looked up to him. He went to Bogan High School, played ball, dressed fly. I started getting good in the neighborhood, so Deion felt I was trying to take his spot. I'm the youngest guy, in sixth grade then. He's in high school.

One day, there's a bunch of kids and I hear footsteps on my porch. There's banging on the door. "Where's Pooh? Tell him to come outside." They're like, "Deion's out there talking shit."

I'm like, "What you mean?" So I go upstairs to get my cousin's new Jordans, squeeze my feet into her shoes, lace them up, and sneak out the house.

When I get to the park it's his older friends and they're like, "Yeah, get him out here." It's like, "I'm gonna kick yo ass!" One on one in front of the neighborhood.

But Little Pooh ends up winning. I loved it. Those are the moments you remember even if it wasn't some big game or tournament. I was so happy, bro, sixth grade, big day for me. But that's also when you start to know something is different, when others in the neighborhood start talking. I'm the only kid playing with the adults. That's also when I first knew there was something else out there besides where I lived.

Sixth grade was when I went somewhere for the first time. I'd started playing AAU and we went to Minnesota. First time ever out of the state. I knew then that things could change. You look on TV, magazines, and you know people are living other lives, but it doesn't seem real. Going to Minnesota and seeing it made it real for the first time. But what can I do? I'm a kid.

Sixth grade also was the first time I went to downtown Chicago, even out of my neighborhood. I played in a championship game at Crane. We got lost driving there and I ended up seeing the skyscrapers up close for the first time.

MY MOM'S NOT RACIST AT ALL. She treats everybody the same, so I never heard the talk about white people. My mom never had to speak with me about race because I guess she kind of realized what type of kid I was. My mom never talked to me about policing or any of that stuff, either. I thank God I was never put in those situations. Mostly lucky, really. My first thing on race, seeing someone racist, believe it or not, was seeing it on *The Jerry Springer Show*.

I remember walking past the TV in my uncle's room. They had the KKK on there. I couldn't understand it. I was like six or seven. I started crying. I thought everybody loved everybody, even though I didn't meet or really speak to a white person until I was in high school. College actually was the first time I was in class with white kids. But I never felt it was any different.

But back home you're seeing people getting pistol-whipped. Hearing gunshots close. You're outside at the park playing basketball or shooting dice, and then you stop for a minute when you hear the shots. You know how far the shots are away from you when you hear them. You hear them so much it gets so you can tell if it's serious or not. You don't run in the house yet. You're so accustomed to it. You know how many blocks it is away. "Okay, that's two blocks out, keep shooting dice." That's what it was in my neighborhood and a lot of neighborhoods.

You ever heard of the culture of violence, like the story of those families in Kentucky—the Hatfields and McCoys—who keep killing each other? It's like what African Americans are kind of stuck in. In my neighborhood, there's no way you could tell me to quit this beef or tell me to stop hating this person when this person killed three of my cousins. That's exactly what's going on, where it's gonna have to take a strong person to turn the other cheek. It's kind of hard doing that with the number of family members who have been lost.

Deion was one of them. He was gunned down at 7:00 in the morning. Because of something his little brother did. My neighborhood, you can't walk around like that. My friend once had to send his little brother to another house for a summer because you can't walk around some places. A boy got killed in my neighborhood a little bit ago because he was wearing AirPods. He didn't even know he was shot when they were shooting at him. He had a twin and they killed the wrong brother. Just the living circumstance. But nobody should have to live like that.

Like in my house. I was getting bit by roaches every night, my mom having to spray them dead around the bed at night while we slept. I'm waking up with roach bites on me. Then having to go to school with roach bites on me. Sweep 'em up and there's another hundred million more. When the crib was getting fumigated one time—I don't know where the fuck we were going, Sears or something to hang out—and we come back and everybody had to team up and sweep up all the roaches.

And now I'm playing chess with friends. I couldn't imagine this at all. I got into gambling in the sixth, seventh grade watching the guys in the neighborhood gamble. I was always at the park, Murray Park, which they'd call Murder Park because of all the shootings. I was at the park so much I don't remember what time the Bulls games came on. I played so much with the older kids, the adults, that's one reason I learned to control the game without shooting. You can't shoot all the time playing with them or they won't let you play.

I remember Reggie saying I got the shooting touch from him, the leaping from Allan, and the ball handling from Dwayne. The speed was me. Reggie used to say it was from running away from his belt.

I DIDN'T KNOW ANYTHING ABOUT THE NBA GROWING UP. I knew we had a team in Chicago called the Bulls and they were somehow just winning. I was always just into the sport. Not any special team. There was never a favorite player. I'll say MJ now when people ask because of what he meant to the sport. But when I was younger I was never glued to the TV when Jordan was playing. And that's no offense to him. It was just off the strength of me loving the sport and me winning a lot at that time.

I also tried tennis once. We had a program at McCormick Place where they let us use their racquets. I was actually winning a lot and got some trophies; Mom has them. But it was too expensive a sport. I played some baseball but our coach was a crackhead. So I figured if he ain't taking it serious, how are the kids gonna take it serious? So I stopped baseball. Basketball you could just go down to the park anytime on your own and hoop.

And then they told me you can get paid to hoop. I really never had thought about that. So I started paying attention to what was going on. One of the people I want to talk about is O.J. Mayo. He really was the guy I was always chasing, the big name. He was the best player I ever saw up close when I was in seventh grade. He was my measure, my Mt. Rushmore of all the players. I always said to myself, "If I can get O.J.," but they kept canceling games between us.

Finally, we played one summer in high school. He had this crazy four-point play to win the game. But as far as chasing something, for me it was always to be better than O.J. Even coming into the league, I was thinking about O.J.

I didn't know I'd feel that way about Bron. I thought it was O.J. until I saw Bron. Then you're like, "Oh shit, it's another level." You get to the league and it's like, even though I was a fan of Bron and had watched him a ton, when you play against him it's a different level.

WE WERE MOVING FROM PAULINA. We lived at 7257 South Marshfield when I was going into seventh grade and then 6701 South Talman for my high school. My grandmother ended up passing and my mom made the move out of our house. By this time my uncles were using drugs a lot. And they didn't have any jobs because there just weren't enough of them where we lived. My mom had to pay all the bills and she got tired of doing that. Me and Allan moved over there with her my freshman year of high school.

I kept gambling to get us money, dice and basketball. I never lost at basketball. The big games they'd put up like $500, $1,000 on me playing. I also pumped gas when I was a kid to get money for my mom and one time for this pet we wanted. Me and one of my friends our senior year, we ended up getting this puppy. His mom didn't really care, so she let us keep the dog. But we didn't have the money to feed him. We were sitting there trying to think about how to get the dog food. I thought, "I'm the light-skinned kid. I'm the most innocent-looking one. If I go to the gas station and ask people, they'll probably give me money to pump their gas." It was just another way to get money for all of us.

I know I said my house was a crack house, and that's true, there were people using drugs, but there's more to it than that. It's, what do they call it, a paradox? My house was the fun place to be. No, not for the drugs, but the kids wanted to be there. I was always trying to get away from my house, like, "No, I wanna leave my house." But with all the other kids it was, "Let's go over to Pooh's house. There's too many rules at my house. Let's go to your house." It was more of what was going on in my house, my mom, the big family. My mom was always playing games, cards. There was always laughter around my house.

But there were two occasions I almost died as a kid. Just dumb shit. This one time with my friend Josh. It was on the

Fourth of July. I lived in the second house from the corner. On the corner is a tow truck. It's been there for like 30 years. We were probably 12 or 13 years old. Josh goes up to the truck, takes the gas cap off, throws a light in the gas tank. Nothing. He lights up another match, throws it in there, a long jet of fire shoots out. Fire all over the place chasing us. Josh's hand is in the fire. I'm panicking like, "What are we gonna tell your mom?" His hand starts to blister up right away, puss and everything. So we had to lie and say that it was a firework that ended up doing that to his hand because we couldn't say that we almost killed ourselves.

The other time was when I drank bleach. Not on purpose like this stuff with Tide Pods you hear about now. Me and my friends, we're outside playing, running around all over, playing tag. I'm running around for maybe 30 minutes. I run into the house to get some water. My mom is doing laundry, so I see the laundry thing on the table. Two big cups. I see the cup and it's clear. I'm in a hurry because the game still is going on. "Gotta get back out." It looked like it's water. I'm like, "Great, Mom left me some water right here. I don't have to pour me a glass of water." I remember drinking it and then waking up with milk on my brow. My mom said I passed out and started throwing up. She called the poison people to see what was going on. They told her to give me milk. The milk made me throw up the bleach. I think I was nine or 10 that time. Dumb stuff you do when you're a kid.

I'M THE YOUNGEST: DERRICK MARTELL ROSE. My mom let my brothers name me and they ended up naming me that, Derrick Martell. They picked out my name. I never asked them why they picked that, not really. The craziest thing about my last name was my mom. That's not really our last name, Rose. My last name is supposed to be Brumfield. My name should be Derrick Brumfield, the way I grew up. That's my mom's maiden name.

She got married to Tommy Rose. She ended up divorcing Tommy, but we kept his last name. Dwayne is the oldest, about 15 years before me, then Reggie about 13, and Allan seven years older. I don't really remember Dwayne being in the house. I remember Dwayne more from my grammar school years, where I would spend the night over at his house.

I don't know who my dad is. I remember asking my mom when I was younger, but you know when people don't want to talk about things, that's when you leave them alone. I kind of let her alone until I got a little bit older, when I could figure out how to express it in a more mature way instead of just coming out straightforward with it. She had a relationship or whatever you wanna call it when she was 34 and she ended up not talking to my dad anymore and he moved out of town. She hasn't heard anything from him since then. I'm thinking he's deceased. I thought he was deceased when I was in high school. Never been contacted once.

So, Tommy Rose was the father in my house. That's the dad of my oldest brother, Dwayne. He's still around, Tommy.

He still goes over to my mom's house in Homewood. We still consider him part of the family. I think my mom divorced all the men she was with, but they still have had a relationship after the divorce as friends.

I don't look at Tommy as someone my mom dated. Tommy was damn near a father figure when I was younger because he was always around. He was the male adult figure who was most around our mom.

She won't be around guys who are bad influences. Tommy's working now, was always working, always had jobs, fought in the Vietnam War. Reggie and Allan, their dad was around, too. His name is also Allan. My mom kept open relationships with all the men. It's actually kind of dope for a female to be doing that. It's kind of different. Remember, she left them. It was for us. I'm also impressed to see how strong she was to stay away from drugs even though her brothers were indulging in that.

Mom came from a rough family from Hyde Park. She dropped out of school when she was a sophomore, had Dwayne when she was like 15. My grandmother told her she wasn't going to help raise him. It was, "This is your responsibility." So from then on my mom tried to get hold of everything and she ended up having my brother. But she was always working to support everyone. She had to drop out of school because of that. Had little b.s. jobs, assistant jobs, secretary jobs at schools. But she'd go weeks sometimes without getting paid because of problems at some of those places. I dealt with that. Imagine feeling that at a young age? I'd be sitting at the table going through bills with my mom, seeing the amount she had and then see it all go away for bills. Trying to process, like, "Damn, how is this possible? Is everybody going through this?"

I was just trying to get hold of what was going on and that's when I kind of got big into gambling. I felt like I had to do something to help for all she was doing.

It was around seventh, eighth grade. I always played basketball. I started playing organized basketball in the fifth or sixth grade. But I would also gamble on basketball. My gambling was like b.s. gambling, where it's shooting dice and shooting jump shots. I never sold drugs in my life. All the guys I grew up with, the guys I consider myself part of, they weren't on drugs. They actually got jobs, went to school, went to college. I was lucky to be around them and to be on the same block. So with the gambling and what I saw my mom going through with the bills, my money became her money.

When I used to win dice games, I would put it in her purse to surprise her. If I ever needed money, it wasn't like I was stealing from my mom. You know what I mean? If I need $20, I'm just gonna grab $20, because I gave her $150 last week. I also was selling the shoes Nike was giving me. That was a big thing. They'd send me shoes all the time. They did that because of my basketball, anytime I'd ask them.

The shoes cost like $250, I'd sell them for $150. You can do whatever you want with them. So I'd wear them a few times and my friends would say, "You done with those Jordans yet?" I'd be like, "Yeah, I'm done with them." That's what my MVP speech was all about. Nothing planned, just realizing what we'd been through and how Mom was always there for me, how we went through everything together. Never even thinking or dreaming it could come out like that:

"Brenda Rose, my heart, the reason I play the way I play, just everything. Just knowing about the days when I didn't feel like I wanted to practice, having all the hard times, waking me up, going to work and just making sure I'm alright and making sure the family's alright. Those are hard days. My days shouldn't be hard because I love doing what I'm doing and that's playing basketball. You keep me going every day and I love you and I appreciate you being my mother."

I just said it. It was something from the heart, how I felt at that moment. It was nothing prepared. Just saw my mom sitting there and thinking back to all she'd done and had to go through for us, and now how much we had. Me seeing her work and hate what she was doing, like not having a career, just having jobs. I didn't have to experience that. I love what I'm doing. My days are different. I shouldn't be complaining, for real, and that's where I was coming from with it. I saw a strong individual—a strong woman—go through something critical, and she's good with it. Good with taking care of her sons, sacrificing for everyone.

That's why I bought her that house the first time I got any money. She saw a house in Homewood she liked. She went to a couple locations and ended up loving a closed-off block. She's nosy, so she can see everything that's going on. Her neighbor's a police officer, so it's perfect for her.

At that time I didn't realize how big it was for her, for everyone really. It was just what you're supposed to do. House for your mom. But the older I got, that's when I realized it was more than that. Because with property—people with wealth know this—you hand things down. That's *our* house now. Can't take it away from us. We could say that. We never had anything to hand down. Now that's our crib where we could sell and do whatever we want with as Roses. We started this. Even living in something like my crib in L.A., coming from where we grew up? We talk about that all the time. We'll be sitting and talking, and people will be crying. Can't believe it, can't believe we're here.

Mom had a lot of friends that she was cool with. She used to play cards a lot. She's a talker. Everybody close to her has been passing and she has to mourn. Two of her younger brothers died from drugs. Her third one is staying with her. You don't know how that's gonna be. Her aunt she used to talk to passed. Her aunt's daughter passed. Three of her sisters passed. She had nine siblings and so many of them passed already. She used to talk to them. That's been her special life. You know, the older you get, the more you want to talk. So my mom is real talkative and sometimes she'll be feeling like she has no one to talk to. It hurts me to see that.

That was always my burden. I was worried not to stress out my mom. "Uh oh, you're stressing your mom, she gonna die early." I was always worried my mom was gonna pass before she saw me achieve anything. I always threw my mom a kiss before games with the Bulls. She was up in the suite and she always said she was throwing it back to me, saying I was her gift from God. She always had this shrine in the basement with all the pictures and stories about me. So growing up I'm like, "I have to play basketball, make it to the next level, pray that my mom can see this." It always was about that.

THE NAME "POOH" CAME FROM MY GRANDMOTHER when I was a baby. In the hood they give you all types of crazy nicknames. I was this fat, yellow, light-skinned baby who used to love sweets. Being chubby they called me "Pooh," like Pooh Bear. Eventually they stopped calling me "Bear" and it was just "Pooh."

At six or seven, I started to lose the fat from running around so much. But I still was into the sweets. Everything you could think of. I used to eat powdered sugar with a spoon and a cup. Straight out, hid it in my dresser drawer to have whenever I wanted. Hey, maybe that's how I got so fast. Watched *Power Rangers* all day on a Saturday just eating sugar. I know, hard to believe now. I loved *Power Rangers*; that was my show.

I've slowed down with the Skittles. After they sent me that Skittles machine when I was with the Bulls, me and my friends ate all the Skittles from the machine. Probably didn't touch another Skittle for like two years. I like Airheads now, Twizzlers, Gushers. My teeth? No problem, they're mostly fake. That's from when Taj Gibson elbowed me that time in training camp and busted my eye. He also chipped about nine of my teeth.

Sixth grade was when I first started to notice there was something different about my basketball. We ended up winning the sixth grade championship at Randolph Magnet School. Randolph only went up to sixth. Like I said, that's when my grandmother died and we moved from Paulina to Marshfield and I had to ride the bus to Beasley Academic Center, where I went for the next couple of years. It was going into high school when we moved to 63rd and Talman. My brother Reggie and his wife were moving, and me, my mom, and another brother moved into Reggie's. I lived in the attic then.

At Beasley we won the seventh and eighth grade championships. My teams won ninth grade, lost 10th. Then won two state titles in 11th and 12th. So you start getting talked about. It's nothing I ever wanted, but it's there when that happens.

But it really was a lot of hard work—a lot. That's where my friend Dre came in. Andre "Dre" Hamlin was older than me, maybe 10 years, but he'd be at the games, courtside sometimes. He was the one taking me to the gym. Kind of that male figure a lot of kids need but don't have. Helping me stay away from the wrong things.

You know that Malcolm Gladwell book about how you need 10,000 hours of practice to master a skill? It's something I thought about. Dre was into gangs, too, but just regular stuff around the neighborhood. He was someone trying to straighten out his life, so he was around the team, helping out, trying to help kids do the right thing and help people and help himself, because he'd been there. He was someone from the neighborhood and I think he could see how hungry I was, that I wanted to get better and better myself as a person. I was mature for my age and I think he knew it was genuine. I knew he didn't have a hidden motive or agenda. There was none of that. I felt he was chasing his dream to straighten out and helping me with my dream became part of that.

Once I got to high school, me and Dre used to work out every day after school. He'd drive us all the way out to Homewood because there was this sports club there. I'd work out and then he'd drive me back home. I never really thought of it like, "Why's he doing that for me?" I always felt he was one of those people who understood you want to get somewhere. I could easily be in the room and you wouldn't even know I was there. But he knew I was trying to be great. He could see it. I felt like he was trying to push me to get there. Maybe because he didn't do what he could have at my age. I don't know. You need people like that in your life. You're lucky if you find them. Especially from my neighborhood.

Dre was the one I talked to a lot. From going to school to the colleges I was thinking about to girls to money, I could ask him questions about anything. I wanted to be the best. At the time, I also began to realize my feel for the game was different than some of the other players. I knew I could change the game, didn't have to score to change the game. I could do it just with my speed, timing, and reaction.

I could go to the gym right now and he'd tell me to do the same-leg layup you see guards doing now. No dribbling. I'd have a hard time doing that. But if you put me in a game and I'm reacting, I'll do it. It's hard to think about for me, it becomes mechanical. That was what no one understood when I was coming back from the injuries, especially the ACL. You have to learn to walk all over again, how to step, everything, and I'm a natural player, instinctive, not thinking about what I do but doing it based on what I see and what the other guy does. But then I'm having to think about even how to walk. Like when I see a hole I'm fast enough to get there, jump high enough to get there.

THE REASON I WENT TO SIMEON HIGH SCHOOL was because of my best friend, Randall Hampton. I got to know him in the sixth or seventh grade. His father ended up bringing him over to our team. And his dad ended up becoming the assistant coach. Randall became the guy who would travel everywhere with me when I was with the Bulls. He traveled with me before the league, too. He's got a trucking company now and we're still close. That's always been my story, stick close to family and your few friends, people you know and trust—you love them, they love you.

I could have gone to other high schools, but you want to be with your guys. Simeon is like a powerhouse basketball school now. I didn't think about that. I wanted to go where it was comfortable. You see a group of guys over there, "What's up?" That's how I wanted to feel. It was like a brotherhood.

What they taught there was discipline, and that's what a lot of us needed at that time, including myself. The discipline was tough, tougher than you'd think or heard, and it still goes on there. But it lets you know the kids want to get better. You get a D, make a selfish pass, you get in trouble. It wasn't always easy because of that, but I agreed to it. I signed up for it. So I couldn't complain.

At Simeon, the best player wears the No. 25 because of Ben Wilson. The number one guy gets to wear No. 25 and then everybody else picks. At freshman orientation they hand you a book about Ben's life story—everything, even about him being killed right outside the school. Ben Wilson would have been one of the best ever. I remember getting the book and reading it, but then being part of that basketball program you hear some of the stories. It's like a myth, this demigod, the stories and how much he achieved. You want to live up to that.

As a freshman, you always wanted to have a big debut game. Everyone always came out to see if the new freshman was all that. I remember going to see Sherron Collins when he was a freshman. I was in eighth grade and I'm thinking to myself, "Damn! He cold. I gotta play against him next year?" He wasn't scoring crazy, but in Chicago, with how many strong players there are, you know a kid can really play if they're able to take on that pressure of being on varsity. He was able to bring the ball up the court comfortably as a freshman. That was rare, but you wanted to be in that rarefied category in Chicago. Some of these guys didn't make it as far as I did, but in high school they were legendary.

Freshman year is tough enough, but it can mess you up even worse when you add having your first love. It was a girl named Marina for me. She actually ended up cheating on me with a guy I knew, a guy whose relative was on our team—a teammate. It broke my heart, for real. I stopped eating, couldn't eat for a week. I didn't cry but I couldn't eat. I was sad as fuck and I just remember with all my relationships that went bad, I used that as material in the gym. "Alright, you cheated on me? I want you to think about this when you see me on TV." Just stupid stuff you think in high school. I know how that sounds now, but that's how you think, how you get through it.

One weird little note from this time, was that I also fell in love with the Range Rover. I know that sounds weird, but I was good friends with Tony Allen's little brother, Ryan,

and when Tony was in the league in Boston he left his little brother his Range Rover. So Ryan used to pick us up in
that Range Rover in high school and I just fell in love with
it. I dreamed it would be something special to have someday. And actually, the first thing I bought when I got money
after being drafted in the NBA—well, after getting my mom
a house in Homewood, where she wanted to be, near friends
and people she knew she could talk to—was a Range Rover.
Of all things, I always wanted a Range Rover. Those were my
dreams. I've been careful with my money, which is first about
having a great team, like a family. My financial advisor and
my banks work together. There's three of them, everybody
watching everybody. Then I link everything. I'm involved, but
I rely on the experts. I invested in trust funds. I don't really
take big risks with money.

Anyway, back to Simeon. We won the city title my freshman year, but I didn't get to go downstate to play for the state
title. The coach then, Coach Hambric, had this rule about no
freshmen on the varsity. I knew he wasn't going to change
his rules for me. There was a chance I could have gone with
them, but he told them they're good without me. It was dis-
appointing, but I had gone to that school because of Randall.
Coach Robert Smith was taking over the next year and he
had seen me play back in sixth grade.

Coach Smith told me back then about how he first
thought Bobby Trimble, one of my teammates in sixth grade,
was the best player because he was scoring all the points. But

he said he realized I didn't have to score. Like when we won my senior year. I think I had two points in the title game. But it made me happy when all the others got the attention. I know I'm a part of it. But I was so happy for them. They'd remember winning that game for the rest of their lives. One thing I had going for me was I felt I already knew what a player was going to do before he did it. That gives you a whole different perspective on the game. I guess that's how I got so many assists.

But I wasn't playing point guard in high school. I played the three. I was doing damn near everything Jabari Parker did later but was doing it at 6'3". It was the same plays he was running, I was running. Down curls, lobs, elbow, isolations. I also could push the ball as a three. We had a decent-sized team, too. Randall was playing point guard. I used to play a way more controlled game. It was in AAU when my brother Reggie switched me to the point guard that I really started to play a totally different game. Like I said, that was when I found my alter ego, No. 1, the scorer.

THAT FIRST GAME MY FRESHMAN YEAR at Simeon was a big one. It was scary. But once I get into the game, it's all gone. We beat Thornwood and then we were off. There were so many fun games—some not so much—battles and rivalries. You're more famous in college, richer in the league, but there's nothing like those high school rivalry games. Eventually you play so many games you start to forget things, but those high school rivalries are unforgettable.

Sophomore year we lost to Bobby Frasor and Brother Rice in double overtime in the sectional. They cheated us. There was a foul call at the free throw line after just about everyone fouled out. It was a hard-fought game. I remember both teams making big plays on both sides, an intense game.

I remember when the draft came and it was me going to Chicago or Miami and I'm thinking, "I'm playing at home or playing in Miami with Dwyane Wade. I can't lose." I never knew Wade as a player, had never heard of him. I'm from the city. I never really saw him there. That's nothing against him, but growing up you heard things about Will Bynum and Sean Dockery, Patrick Beverley, Sherron Collins, and that white boy who went to Glenbrook North, Jon Scheyer. Real battles, but sorry, no D-Wade, as good as he became.

My junior year, when we won the city title, the battles were serious. Scheyer averaged like 50 the last four games, but we ended up winning against his team. Patrick Beverley, man, he was something. You see how tough he is in the league now, doesn't back down from anyone. The better you are, the tougher he challenges you. That's what the high school games are like. Bragging rights over fame. We played against John Marshall High—which we just called Marshall—and Beverley, an exhibition game once at Chicago State, and they beat us by 20. It wasn't close. They smacked us by 20 and he's talking some big shit, same way he does now. But it was even worse then. Oh my god, smacked us by 20 and then we end up playing them for state.

I don't know if you know this but because of some weird high school stuff they make the two city teams play against each other so there's not two Chicago teams playing downstate for the title. That was the year we beat Peoria Richwoods in a low-scoring game for the title, Simeon's first since 1984.

Beat Scheyer and Glenbrook North that year. Scheyer was a hooper. We knew that when we played against them that it was gonna be the hardest game of the tournament. I remember our whole team having to always be aware of where he's at. I think one game he had like 50 in a half. Lots of city kids think white kids can't play. But when you play AAU, you go everywhere else and it opens your eyes to everything. Then you get home and you don't tell nobody that, "This boy from Iowa kicked my ass." I keep that on the hush.

I don't judge anybody on their look or color or name. If you're on the court, I'm giving you respect and that's that. It's why the basketball court is such a good place. The world should be like that. Play everyone straight up and then shake hands. Going out we knew how we had to play them because all the guys played AAU and we knew what type of guys we were playing against. We knew what he was capable of.

Then it was Marshall. We ended up beating them and I remember walking up to Beverley like, "Good luck in college." His high school career was done. It was his last game. He was a senior. Sweet after the way they got us. That's the kind of rivalry thing you love in high school. That was the kind of trash talking I like. I don't talk to guys in games. I like to talk about the final score.

I remember a game when we beat Morgan Park—that was scary. We're walking out of the gym and there's these guys with ski masks over their faces waiting for us to come out. We're at their school, so there's a lot going on after the game. A fight breaks out. I'm seeing everybody scattering everywhere, everybody punching people, kicking people. So somehow you just end up fighting. I was with Randall. Next time I saw him he was holding his nose, his mouth busted, just a crazy night. But that was life in the Public League sometimes, too. You go at each other so hard it can spill over.

I ONLY PLAYED ON TWO AAU TEAMS—Mean Streets Express and my old team, Ferrari. My brother organized Mean Streets after I left Ferrari. It was basically my team. He wanted me to have a platform. Reggie didn't want to start from scratch and start a new AAU team, so he went to a team in Mean Streets that already existed. He said, "Look, I've got my brother and he's a hell of a player. Can you start a B team?" If you're good, they support you, but if not everything just dries up.

The backcourt on that Mean Streets team was me and Eric Gordon Jr. We won Peach Jam, which is one of the biggest AAU tournaments in the world. And we were the first team to ever do that our first year being in the tournament.

When it was time for college we almost both went to Indiana. He decommitted from Illinois and I was about to go to Indiana with him. I was this close and just talking to my mom, but she was like, "Just sleep on it and tomorrow you'll wake up and know what to do." I woke up and Memphis was where I felt more comfortable.

North Carolina had always been my dream school to go to. Bobby Frasor was one reason. With him going there it showed me at the time, "Damn, they're looking at kids here." You know what I mean? I was looking at it like if they were looking at Bobby, they probably saw me play. So I was thinking maybe I could go there.

The first letter that I ever got from a college was from UConn. Yeah, exciting. I hung it up in my room. Recruiting was crazy, but not so bad for me. My brother was taking care of all the meetings. But stuff would happen. I remember being at a party downtown during that time. We were staying the night over at the Hyatt and I remember waking up and my phone was going crazy. My brother was like, "Hey, get back to the house!"

So I hurry back to the house in the middle of the night. Some white guy had jumped out the car—it's when we were living on Talman—and he's asking my sister-in-law why Eric Gordon took Illinois off his list. She was scared, thought he was trying to harm her. So she called my brother and said someone was attacking her. She said somebody was there, offering, talking about paying money.

But not Coach Calipari. He made it simple and easy. For one, he came to my house. Bruce Weber from Illinois never would. Cal was the first coach to actually pull up at my house. Pulled up in a Hummer and everything. I didn't even know where Memphis was. Didn't have family down there or anything. But I went on the visit and got a sense of what was going on with his system and I felt I could just fit in with the older guys.

I liked North Carolina from watching TV, the Duke–North Carolina games, the legacy of North Carolina. So you wanna go there. My list was North Carolina, UCLA, Indiana, Kansas, Memphis, DePaul, and Illinois.

My brother didn't want me to visit UCLA or North Carolina. I think he thought I'd commit right away. He wanted me to think and make the decision. He really put me in position to have control over my life, not the other way around. People always think my family made decisions for me. I was always too stubborn for that.

When I was younger, I was obsessed with North Carolina. Told everyone I was going there. What got me with Illinois was Bruce Weber wouldn't come to my crib. I probably wouldn't have gone there, but I think he was scared to come to my house because of the neighborhood. That's what it looked like to me, so they were off my list. It became, "Why do I always have to go see you?" I used to sneak off to Illinois sometimes to play. But if you won't come to my crib?

Cal was the biggest reason I went to Memphis.

He's got that gift of gab. But he also was honest to me. He told my mom I was going to do what I had to do or wouldn't be in his program for long. I respected him for treating my mom the way he did. He treated her like he'd known her for 20 years. It was with utmost respect and for me to see a white guy being honest like that meant something.

I didn't grow up around white people. My first time being in class with a white kid was in college. So a white dude coming in my crib and talking to my mom and she's understanding where he's coming from and he's showing her respect, that was big. And I was feeling the same way. He stood on everything he said. He has integrity. That's something I respect about him.

I know what some people say about Cal, but he was always just honest with me: "If you don't do what you're supposed to do, you won't be in my program long, kid." If I hadn't gone to Memphis, it probably would have been Indiana. I really didn't know I was gonna commit to Memphis until I went down for the visit. It just felt so much like home.

They had older guys, more mature. There was focus. It seemed everybody had one goal, one mission. When I got back home, my mom told me to sleep on it. She was like, "I don't wanna know right now. Make your decision in the morning." I slept on it and I was really debating going to Indiana. I knew E.J.—that's what we call Eric Gordon Jr.—was going there. That was real big. I woke up and Memphis was the only thing that was on my mind and I went downstairs and told her. She was kind of surprised. But she knew I was in good hands. And we made it all the way to the championship game.

JUNIOR YEAR IN HIGH SCHOOL was that first championship for Simeon in so long. Like I said, it was a low-scoring game, like 31–29, and I won it with the last shot. Tie game and they're taking the ball out. The guy who was next to me, Dex, he was our harassing guard, the best defensive guard we had. He ends up getting a steal off the inbound. He gives the ball to me like it's a handoff in a football game. I remember being nervous at first, doing a hop like, "Let's go."

I remember later Coach Smith saying he turned to the bench and said we were winning, just the way I took that hop and my look. But in reality, I was scared. Kind of like that Mike Tyson thing when he was scared about getting into the ring. Until you do it a certain amount of times, you're gonna be nervous. I don't have that now, but when I was younger I did.

After I did the hop, it went away. I'm like, "I gotta make a move." And by that time I was already in my mode of attacking and trying to get to a shot. When I took that bounce, it's like, "Damn, we got it. It worked." There's nothing like that, when you make a clutch shot, execute a play, or make an easy layup. Taking the hop was just the confidence that I was gonna do something.

I remembered seeing what kind of defense they were playing. They were playing zone throughout the whole game. Of course, I'm gonna go left. I'm a right-hand driver who goes left. That shot was the same shot I made with the Bulls when we beat the Lakers on Christmas in 2011, the first game after the lockout, a floater. I'm thinking back then, if I get inside it could be a floater and there's a good chance it's going in.

Senior year, we're downstate again, which is great, but I'm also thinking about Shaun Livingston, how he got *two* state championships. In Chicago, they always tell you about the people ahead of you. You're always chasing. So, "Man, we have to get two. Be the first city player to have two."

We got that one and then there were a lot of the big individual matchup games that season. There was Oak Hill and we beat Brandon Jennings' team, lost that one in Vegas to O.J. Mayo, lost in Madison Square Garden against Kemba Walker's team. That was the game I passed for a last shot and our guy missed. It was my fault. I'm the senior. I have to take that shot. Like when we lost to Kansas in the championship game when I was at Memphis. I remember putting my hand up. I missed a free throw, it's on me.

Cal would tell me there's no way. But I never shied away from anything like that. Bad play, bad mistake. I feel like I learn from my mistakes, but I made one like that again later with the Bulls. It was the playoff game in Milwaukee in 2015. We ended up winning the series, but I cost us a game. Jason Kidd was coaching the Bucks and drew up a play when Jerryd

Bayless made a layup at the end. It was on me. I knew it. But that's also one of the reasons why now I'm a better free throw shooter. That's from that miss with Memphis. I always remember the mistakes more than the game-winners. The losses seem to stand out even more. Every summer I try to improve because of games when you miss and it costs your team. But what fun.

It also helps prepare you for the other stuff. We were winning so much in Chicago in high school it was kind of like what the fans did to me with the Bulls toward the end of my career, the negative. They did that to me in high school, too, because we were winning too much. I remember talking to my teammates in high school, it became us against the world. You see all those people celebrating against you. It's tough, but it happens. I had it with the Bulls. No one wants to be booed in their hometown. I remember it happening overnight with LeBron after he went to Miami, and thinking how sad it was to see someone in their hometown having people turn on you. Then I started thinking about how I would deal with it.

Then I was dealing with it. Sometimes not so good.

THE SAT CONTROVERSY WAS PART OF HIGH SCHOOL. Everyone has already drawn conclusions on it one way or the other. It hurt most because the guys were affected, my teammates at Memphis, when the NCAA took the wins away. Living through the scrutiny also gave me a perspective on how the college entrance system can discriminate in certain ways.

I passed the first semester at Memphis with no problem, no help. I was just going to hoop, ready for it. I always passed my classes in high school. I never had a problem. I had over a 3.0 GPA one semester, I think. Got one F ever. I'm thinking, "I'm going to the league. I'm not going for a degree, but someone's making a lot of money on this."

But it's, "He's stupid, he's this, he's that."

One semester. Without nobody, I got it done. My grades always were good. The reality for me and many other kids coming from our situations was there wasn't test prep like in other places. Our schools are not always set up to prepare you for college entrance. You always hear those kinds of tests discriminate because schools are different. Simeon was no b.s. We were taking the classes. But I *need* to get to college in order to get to the NBA. That's how players like me see it.

So what was going on? Making money off these kids coming in to play ball? Exploitation? Come on, man. I wanted to say something in Chicago when I was going through this and just rant about them doing that. "What you're doing is wrong, period. There's rules they had a long time ago that don't make no sense now." Back then the colleges didn't have billion-dollar contracts with the networks to televise their games. And where did those billions go? What are they doing with that money? Not going to the players. Not going to the next generation of players to help them prepare for entering college.

What about the school? The money is not going to the school, either. If that was the case the landscape would be totally different. It would be more scholarships, free tuition. Maybe all these kids who aren't in sports wouldn't have to pay so much to go to college. But does the money go there?

I think it's important for people to know that when I went to school, I did my work. I'm not saying I was the smartest, but I was getting steady Cs, an A, a B. Had some great teachers.

Like where I got my love of history—and conspiracies. Mrs. Brinkley and Mrs. Harley in high school were special. Mrs. Brinkley taught African American history. But in her classes she used to go on lectures about the government, like how they had cameras and TVs everywhere. I remember before they had them, her telling us about how they're going to have these big, flat TVs on the wall, and they're going to have cameras in them and you better watch out because people, the government, can watch you. I didn't know what to believe. It didn't sound right, but it was a fun story to hear. I didn't take it too seriously, but like a lot of people, I like to talk about conspiracies. Recently I saw this story about China putting things in TVs or computers where they can track you. Is it true? I don't know. Probably not. It sounds like a good story, though.

Mrs. Brinkley ended up passing away with cancer. But people like that are special for your life. They make you think, start to examine the world, challenge you to think for yourself. She was the first teacher who really caught my attention in class. I didn't know I loved history. But it was just the way she was explaining it, making it come to life, keeping you up on what was going on, telling you stories, and allowing you to expand your mind.

Just think about what we had to go through and what others like me were going through every day. I'm coming into school and you ask me about a national test? I got attacked by roaches last night. I'm itching right now taking this test. Like, how can I focus on school sometimes when I'm trying to think about how to survive in bed at home?

I love the fact that in the mornings now with my son we can have an argument about what he's going to eat, pancakes or waffles. You didn't get breakfast options where I grew up. "All we have is toast." So I'm lucky and grateful for what my son can have, living and caring and loving and not having to worry. There'd be numerous times on the porch when people would pull up with clubs, bats, shit you see in the movies. Being in the crib, that shit traumatizes you. A kid shouldn't have to go through that.

I always felt like if I passed the last exam, I was fine. That showed I paid attention to everything, meaning I could do the work—and I did. Basketball was too important to not take the work seriously. If I passed that exam it shows I wasn't bullshitting anyone. And I was passing. Okay, I didn't always do my homework. But I was okay in class. Teachers would give me Ds because of the homework thing sometimes. It was, "Hey, you smartass, gonna give you a D because you didn't do the homework, but you can do the exam."

Homework never had a shot against basketball. Come in, put my book bag down, go right outside, go to the court, shoot by myself, shovel the snow by myself if there's snow. If there's a dice game, head over to shoot dice, or pump some gas for cars because we need the money. And I'm doing that by myself until my mom comes home, sometimes waiting at the game to walk me back home. That was my life.

Look, without the one-and-done rule, I would have been in the league. I was going there the next year. You think I was the only one? At first, I wasn't sure if I'd be at Memphis just one season, but Cal during that season was like, "I'm gonna hand the team over to you, play the way that you normally play and we'll follow." And then everybody started playing. The only thing I was worried about was just getting to college, start playing, just get through that first semester and I'm good. That was my mindset. I was going to the league.

I NEVER REALLY HAD ANY BIG RACIAL STUFF, any fights like that, but you feel it, the silent racism when you're black going into places. Like when I couldn't buy that building in downtown Chicago for my girl to open a shop. Didn't want black people coming in there. They can't say so, but you know that's what that's about. I had one thing happen at Memphis—it was no big deal, but still, it shows you something about the country.

I was walking back to my dorm at Memphis early on and there was a pickup truck with three or four white boys in it. I remember them just riding real slow behind me. They said it softly at first, like, "What's up, my nigga?" I think there were three or four of them laughing, maybe to see my reaction. I'm acting like I didn't hear 'em. I kept walking and one said it louder, "What's up, my nigga?" I heard him again. I just looked at him and I kept walking, because me just coming from Chicago, we don't bullshit. Like, if you're trying to start something, then start something. So I just kept walking and left it like that. That really was the only thing I ever experienced there.

I never said anything to anyone, but you know those guys saying those things to me in Memphis aren't coming to Chicago, to my neighborhood. It's why racism is like being a coward—being tough in a gang. We have those guys in Chicago, just that they're killin' each other.

I've had other things like that, but I laugh at them. Let you know I understand it, but I always take the higher road whenever I see racism, because I feel like they're dark souls. It's energy I don't need to be around. I'm not gonna say nothing because it's four or five of y'all against one. I'm just gonna keep walking.

I look at y'all faces, though. So if I see one of y'all walking one day without your protection…you know. But I never had something where I was involved in a fight. It is kind of hard keeping your mouth shut, though, when you see things like police brutality, even if so many good officers are mixed in with the bad ones.

I WAS ALWAYS PROUD TO BE IN MEMPHIS once I started to learn more about it. Of course, they have the National Civil Rights Museum there because that's where Martin Luther King Jr. was assassinated. But that was where he was working for his people, supporting the garbage workers who were striking for a fairer situation. Another great African American man, a man who cared for others and sacrificed, sacrificed himself, really. It makes me think of Arthur Ashe, who was one of my heroes. Tragic the way he died so young.

The closest teammate I've had—other than Randall in high school—was Joakim Noah, and that's where Arthur Ashe comes in again. A lot of people don't mess with Joakim because they think there's some bad shit that comes with him or just how outspoken he is or whatever. For me, I can respect that, knowing everything about him, like for him to be who he is and act the way he is. It's an amazing story behind it. I actually want my son PJ to grow up to be like Joakim. You know, a free spirit, a loving guy. Joakim loves people. He's just a great role model. And his story is special.

His pops was discovered by Arthur Ashe when he was just a kid—took him from their family and put him in school, a tennis school. So I'm asking Jo one day, "Your pops really knew Arthur Ashe?" I had played tennis and was pretty good and Arthur Ashe was such a hero if you were African American and played tennis, so off that, you got me. Joakim's pop got put in school—they told his family he'd be taken care of and the family agreed to it. This is a stranger taking your kid, just historic.

And think of Jo. To be this silver-spoon kid, his dad is a big star, rich and famous, and he don't want nothing to do with that. Like, "Nah, I'm doing my own thing." Gets multiple contracts by himself when he easily could have lived off of his pops forever. His pops could've got him jobs. But he didn't want that. He's got his own individuality. That's what I love about Jo, how he created something on his own. I want that for my son, too. I ask Jo questions so I can hear how he acted when he was young to get that way. Just so I can figure it out as a father with PJ when he's doing shit he isn't supposed to be doing. Jo tells the truth about what he experienced. He probably don't even know how deep I think about it, but I love how open he is, how he trusts me with certain things.

Arthur Ashe was in a sport where they didn't even want him in there. That's the kind of inspiration that drives me. First off, to even play that sport, you gotta have money. So how are you that good to even know this? You know what I mean? He was great. And even more than that, he cared about people. He was on his way, doing his own thing, trying to change the world, and those are the things I respect about him. Then he gets HIV and all he cares about is helping others to learn all about the disease, marching for civil rights, his work with South Africa and apartheid—what a great, great man.

I used to talk to Jo all the time about his dad at Wimbledon and Ashe and that led to us having conversations about Africa, the world, civil rights—we hardly ever talked about basketball. We talked about immigrants a lot—his mom is from Sweden. Talked about the health care problems here. I felt like everything Arthur Ashe was doing was perfect. He was

Little Pooh

Me and my mom

*Me and my brother
Allan*

*Broken arm,
still hoopin'*

*Me and my friend
Bubble*

Simeon. I wanted to live up to the honor of wearing No. 25.

Simeon team, 2005

Taking the ball from Jon Scheyer in the Illinois state playoffs. He was a hooper.
(AP Images)

After the shot to beat Peoria Richwoods for the state championship. That's Randall Hampton next to me. (AP Images)

Coach Cal made it feel like I had a home at Memphis. (AP Images)

Layup against UCLA in the Final Four. (AP Images)

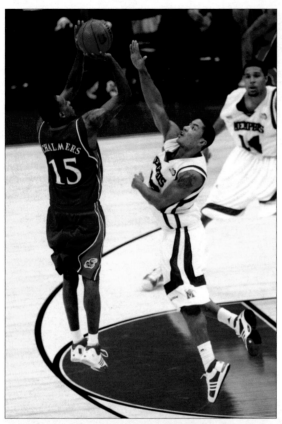

Fucking Mario Chalmers hitting a three-pointer to send the championship game to overtime. (Bob Donnan— USA TODAY Sports)

When people ask me about my biggest disappointment in basketball, I say it's losing to Kansas in the championship game. (AP Images)

All of a sudden, I had all these NBA reporters around me and asking me questions. I'm an introvert; I wasn't prepared for it at all. (AP Images)

Our house on Paulina.

All love after getting drafted by the Bulls. (AP Images)

helping people. Dope in tennis. Dies at like 50, going in for an operation and he comes out dying of AIDS. Why him?

Those are the people you hear about and you know you can't give up.

MY SEASON IN NEW YORK WAS TOUGH, and I know I fucked up by going home that one time without telling anyone first. That's on me. It's one of the reasons I've had to take these minimum contracts. I know what some teams think about me because of that. It's okay—it's on me. Again, something I have to show. But that season in New York we got to go to the new African American museum when we were in Washington, a special tour before it opened.

I still get emotional when I think about it. I rarely break down and cry. Other than when my grandmother died, my knee that time in the hospital, not much. Maybe when BJ called to tell me that the Bulls had traded me to the Knicks. But it got me at that museum. Sometimes I'll be telling someone about it and start crying, trying to catch my breath. Amazing.

You walk in that place and, for me, you get emotional just being there. Because you're surrounded by greatness—true greatness—but how they had to suffer and never got fair chances, it hits you, because they always tried to hide that story. Native Americans, African Americans, the embarrassment for our country to treat people like that. You get a close-up look into these people and see how hard they worked and how they were treated.

It's emotional and it motivates me.

I saw Nat Turner's Bible, the female slaves and how they didn't have anything to write with or on—if the masters saw them writing they would kill them. So they used to pull out their hair and sew it into cloth. The thing that stood out—and I still start shaking when I think about it—is the auction block. Selling people. You feel me? I get to show my talent and play basketball, but look what these people went through, a whole country built on that. And it went on for so, so long and they were still making laws after the Civil War to make it like slavery—can't vote, lynchings, all that.

How are you great when you can't confront your truth? That's America?

I'm not even there, but I totally understand it. It's something I hold in because I don't talk to people about that. But it helped show me who I am. Look around even today, even with me. I have money but when I shop—I'll be in certain stores and just because of my appearance, especially now with my hair longer, little bit of hair on my face—I'll be around a white person and I can feel the vibe that they're scared. You hear these stories on the news of people calling the police because they saw a black person near their house. Really?

I can be in a store and the people at the door, security, they don't know who I am. I walk in and might be looking like a bum because I look like a bum a lot of the time—or looking reckless after I came from a workout—and I'm not that tall, I look regular. They don't think I'm supposed to be in there and they'll follow me around the store. Keep following me, watching to see if I touch anything, like, "He ain't gonna try something on! Oh no!"

And then it's, "D-Rose, that you?"

I laugh at it, but it is serious and it still says something about our country. It also gives me an insight into what's going on. It's stereotyping, but I can't let things like that affect me. Can't get mad at everyone. Hey, if you feel that way, it's on you. You got the problem. But can I get these shoes?

That's also what I love about my family. They're not into the things I'm into. I'm into materialistic things even though I don't look like it a lot. I can't help that. My family ain't into none of that. I'm into clothes. I want the $150 shirt, but not them. That's why I love just being around them, because when you're around that NBA circus all the time, you can get caught in that matrix and think that's how life really is.

I am into fashion even though I don't wear the clothes a lot. I'm a hoarder. I get a collection, like a brand collection, but I just keep it. So like, get it and wear it, but then keep it for years, just look at it. Then I love when I wear those old clothes years later and another dude who is into fashion will be like, "Damn, you kept that that long?" I love when people notice that.

I love my stuff to be basic, too. My stuff don't say Gucci on the back. I want my stuff to be kind of hidden. My style?

I love the laid-back look, but I can be flashy sometimes. I don't dress like Russell Westbrook, but I'll wear a simple outfit where the shoes will be loud. I let the shoes do all the talking. Shoes will be bright or match with the shirt. Or the shirt will be loud and the bottom will be quiet. Simple jeans, simple shoes, but the shirt is talking. Outfits like that. It's how I show my personality. Quiet, but not really. Also depends how I feel, how the day is going. Happy, bright, loud, spending time with my kids. If it's dark, what's the point of putting on certain clothes? I've got suits. Just got nine new suits. I wear my suits to my bank meetings.

Clothes are the only thing I really like to spend on. NBA guys have money. I know guys who would spend $150,000 on a watch and a chain. I might spend that, but more like on the trip I took in summer 2018 with my family, about a dozen of us to New York for a J. Cole concert. I love seeing that talent—it's empowering and inspiring for me, shows the hours he put into his craft. Have to respect that. But also when I do something for myself with the money, it's more like that, the experience everybody gets. That makes me feel good. We can all talk about this later on down the line and reminisce, like we've done with other concerts we went to. We had a blast at the concerts. We enjoy it. It's priceless times—you can't buy that.

There's nothing wrong with buying the watch or chain. Don't get me wrong. Everybody's got they own poison. I'd rather keep that money than spend it if I'm an average Joe.

I've saved a lot. Worked hard enough, so I can do it some-times. I don't really have extravagances, other than the clothes. I do have a collection with Adidas with a brand. Later on down the line I want to put out a brand with women's clothes, like Stella McCartney. Most of the people I go with over-seas to China are women. But I can't love fashion over hoo-pin' right now. Hoopin' is number one now. I've gotta give it my all because of my kids.

I NEVER WANTED TO EMBARRASS MY MOM, so I hated it when a pic-ture came out from Memphis when I was with the Bulls, that I was flashing a Gangster Disciples gang sign. I wasn't actu-ally making a gang sign, but that's the way it looked.

I love kids and believe it's the youth who drive the world. I want to be on the right side of that, one of the models. They're gonna see bullshit. They notice it right away. They're gonna tell you the truth. And my thing is always to lead by example. Which is why the gang sign thing was all wrong, but really, that wasn't what it was about.

I was doing that to say, "Hey, we're number one in Memphis." Me throwing up that sign was me saying, "Hey, Pooh is ballin' in Memphis." Like, we're in Memphis, all the way from Chicago, number one. Be proud from Chicago. That's all. But it was totally the wrong way to do it.

It hurts if you're trying to lead by example. I learned a big lesson. But it's a lesson to them, too: don't go in that direction.

They can see that I'm not perfect and they see somebody who's trying to do his best, but he can make a mistake. But don't make a big one. I always regretted that.

Anything I got caught up in that wasn't the right thing, I regretted. Even with me having the attitude I did in Chicago when I was being criticized so much in the media. The whole way I handled that situation, I should have been the bigger person, but I was too young at the time.

Was it fair? Doesn't matter. You have to handle it the right way. I didn't. The hate is easy to see. Like when I came back with Cleveland and Shaquille O'Neal and Charles Barkley and all them on TNT tried to say I was done, that my career was over and I should just leave. You could see the hate. But I keep hoopin' because people are gonna hate. Kids are going to have that stuff happen to them, where there's jealousy and hate, and I want to be someone who sets an example.

Then with all of them it was, "Hold up, D-Rose had a hell of a playoff series in 2018." "Hold up, D-Rose is putting up numbers in '19." Now what the fuck are they talking about? Are you thinking about basketball? Or is it personal? Everyone needs to learn to deal with that stuff.

SO, NO, I DIDN'T STAY LONG IN COLLEGE, but I definitely learned there. Memphis was a great time. Had a great season, great teammates, Cal. But mostly, I was so proud of myself, the way I handled my responsibilities being on my own for the first time. I had to get through that semester and I did the work, got the grades. Not in any trouble, on time, always where I was supposed to be. Going to class, dedicating myself to the sport. I know it doesn't sound like a lot, but it showed a lot for me. I was in the gym a lot. That kind of saved me from acting out or being in the crowds where you got in trouble.

There were a couple of bar fights before I got there with the players, teammates—it's a Southern place. Cal put out a statement; Twitter barely existed at that time. He came out on the news saying to email him if you saw anyone from his team out. Said to MySpace him if they saw us in the club or whatever. Most guys would go out in Mississippi, anyway, across the river, if they went out. He was on us all the time to be right.

For me, it was the three Gs: Girls, Gym, Games. That's how I stayed away from it. I never was a guy being out, anyway. Which is what later made it so weird to be attacked like I was in the media. The thing that hurt was being around my family and hearing people slander my name. My family knows who I am. They know I'm not aggressive. And to just hear somebody kill you like that. It hurt 'em. No one thinks about that part. Probably why that anger and that aggression came back when I was in Chicago. It didn't feel right because I felt like I had to defend not only myself, but my family.

Back at Memphis, it was such a special time, a special season. We started out 26–0 and were number one. Small place and no one expected it and we're dominating. Big games, too.

We went to New York and beat my guy O.J. Mayo in over-time. What I remember is the way we were rolling. Every game we played it felt like we were unbeatable and we felt like Cal was controlling the team perfect.

Cal's got ways of motivating, and one was he knew that all of us loved money. So he'd be yelling, "Ka-ching! Ka-ching!" as we're going through games. Talking about the draft, the lottery. I believe that had we lost a game in the tournament before we went to the championship, I wouldn't have been the first pick in the draft. I think Michael Beasley would have been number one. When we got to the tournament, though, Cal turned it up for me.

He called me into his room before the tournament started. We're talking about how I feel, having a regular conversa-tion, when out of nowhere he was like, "Kid, you know we're gonna want you to play the way you normally play or we won't have a chance."

What he meant was, play the way I played in AAU. Cal rarely came to my high school games. He recruited me because of what he saw in AAU. When he went to my high school games, he was like, "What the fuck is this? You're not play-ing point guard. You don't got the ball in your hands. We're changing that."

It was shocking for me to hear him say it because it's the only time he talked about me taking over the team or some-thing like that. Normally, he had conversations with Chris Douglas-Roberts, because Chris was older. He'd depend on him because he was here before me. To hear him say that, yeah, I had to act like I was ready for it and take responsibility. I was surprised. But I delivered and it worked out.

Cal was great to play for. Still keeps up with me. He also motivated you by throwing out a little bit of history sometimes. I liked that. He'd always throw out stories about old players and how hard they worked, how much they appreciated the game. Also, he was always making the team feel like it was us against everyone else. He was huge on that. No matter what was going on the whole year, we felt like we were fighting everybody. We were number one throughout the season and that was the reason why. They had to recognize us. Maybe they didn't want to, but we'd make 'em. That was another thing that drove us from this school no one ever talked about. But I knew how good the team was. I saw it firsthand. I didn't care about what people said. I practiced with them. I saw them up close. This is similar to the teams I normally played with, like in Chicago, too, not a bunch of big names.

We lost that one game before the tournament against Tennessee in overtime. Honestly, we just never thought we'd lose the way it was going that season. We were up most of the first half. It was a surprise. We thought we were gonna win every game we played. They just played a perfect game that night. Playing so much basketball, some nights it will be like that. Just one of them nights.

Then there was the championship game, losing to Kansas. That was probably my biggest disappointment in basketball. When people ask me, that's the game I say that about. It was me missing a free throw that cost us. Putting my hand up. It was on me.

When I was younger, I won all those championships and it seemed like my teams were always gonna win. You think it's gonna continue in college. Then you make it all the way to the dance and it's like, "I'm about to do this, too." Going into that game I was like, "Yeah, going to do my thing, we got this." We're up, I make a three, but they change it to a two when I had that run going late, scoring 14 of 16 Memphis points.

We're up and it looks like we've got it. Chris goes up there and misses free throws. I go up there, miss a free throw, too, and fucking Mario Chalmers hit that three-point shot. Even before that, Sherron Collins, Chicago guy from Crane, hit a big shot and I felt then, "Alright, we get to overtime and we should be fine." But by that time, we let the game slip and it was over. I played all 45 minutes.

I just remember walking off the floor and the fireworks were burning me on the way out. Being so mad. Anybody that touched me, I felt like I was gonna fight 'em. People cheering. There was a lot going on and I was confused, emotionally distraught. But Cal, I remember him afterward telling us, "Man, I thank you guys for everything y'all did. We made it to the championship, which nobody thought we were gonna make it to. We had the number one spot until we lost to Tennessee."

We weren't a good free throw shooting team, but we always said we'd make the big ones when we had to, like Shaq always said. He didn't most of the time, we didn't that time. Taught me, at least, the importance of free throws. It's something I saw with Magic Johnson, also. Check his free throws and how much better he got. Shooting 90 percent by his last season. It became something for me to go right away and practice. Right after that loss. So I never shot free throws again as low as I did in college. Was up to like 86, 87 percent after my injuries, getting better just about every season.

I missed one free throw in that game, so the truth is if I had hit the free throw, I probably wouldn't have worked on improving that part of my game. I was telling Cal about the game and I was like, "My bad, my bad."

He was like, "Go through the tape, Derrick. We could have lost this game through this play, that play." I appreciated him saying that. But it was on me. It was tough because I had never been on a team like that where we were that close, super close, like in high school. They were kind of older guys, but for me to come in there and click like that made it like a family. I loved that, making it feel like home.

And the crazy thing was I was about to do something I never thought I would—go back to Chicago to play for my hometown team.

I WAS NEVER THINKING ABOUT PLAYING FOR THE BULLS. I really wasn't a fan of any team growing up. Don't get me wrong, I was glad for them, and they were always making the playoffs, but I was just thinking about my games. I wasn't watching them. Watched the league, you know, just to see who I have to ball against. Then the Bulls missed the playoffs in 2008 and got like a 1 or 2 percent chance of winning the lottery, so I'm not thinking much about playing back home.

Then they get the first pick.

But I wasn't really thinking about being number one. For a long time at Memphis I'd been thinking maybe it would take me two years to get to the league. Then the tournament and everything happened. They were telling me the Bulls wanted a guy who could score better, which I figured meant Michael Beasley. You heard they didn't want guys from Chicago, like it was too much pressure to play at home. Someone said that's why they didn't take Michael Finley years earlier, and he became an All-Star.

Pat Riley and the Heat had the number two pick and I knew Riley liked me. So I wasn't sure what was going to happen. With D-Wade, they could use a point guard. Nobody in my family would have felt bad if I would have gone to Miami. To me it was the same: Chicago? Miami? Win-win. That's how I felt. Win because I'm playing at home or win because I'm playing in Miami with D-Wade.

The Bulls had Kirk Hinrich. I heard they weren't sure right up until before the draft.

And then I was thinking, "Don't pick me."

You know how you're in New York right before the draft and they call you and let you know they're gonna draft you? You gotta act surprised that night, but come on. They're saying I was going number one or whatever, but the night before I remember eating in New York with my agent, BJ Armstrong. BJ hands me the phone. I'm talking to Gar Forman and the others and they start bringing up my brother's past. "Your brother, he was locked up for this, that, whatever."

I know teams do all this research, but I didn't understand, because it's like, "Are you drafting me or my brother?" My brother didn't have anything to do with what I do on the court. I just remember getting up and getting out of there— mad. At the table mad and then I'm outside and everybody's confused like, "Derrick, what's going on?"

I'm telling BJ to tell them, "Don't pick me then, I'm going to Miami. If they're worried about what's going on with my brother's life, that's something I didn't know nothing about. I don't go into my brother's file. I don't know about that." I love my brother. I don't care about that.

Then they picked me.

It hurt, but it was all behind me once they drafted me.

I WASN'T WORRIED ABOUT PLAYING IN CHICAGO, even if some people said there's a lot of distractions. I never hung around with that many people. The people I hang around with are the same people I've been hanging around with since sixth grade. That's why I say it all goes through my friends, and the people I always kept close to me are the people I know I can trust, the people still with me. When they were talkin' shit about me in the media it would trickle down to them, so that was really the hard part for me.

My biggest thing being in Chicago was me not having the freedom to do what I wanted, the boundaries that popped up. I can't go places and just be normal, do normal things. When I look back, I also think one problem with playing in Chicago was I wasted too much energy. Playing in my hometown, there was no way around it. When you step outside, you got people looking at you crazy. It's either they're looking at you crazy or with excitement. It became a circus, but outside of that I could have dealt with it.

There was one big thing about playing in Chicago, and I thought that was going to lead to a championship. I never stopped believing that. What did it take MJ? Seven years, he was chasing. I was always chasing. Going back, I knew that was gonna push me to play great basketball. That's how I took it. Playing in Chicago, being judged all the time on everything, being compared to Michael, that would push me, push us. Me being judged against the greats who came before, that's the way it always was for me, and we were always winning, so it was good. It was a continuation of the pressure. It never got to me.

Well, until the end.

It was only at the end—that last year with the Bulls—I felt the city was changing on me. You're in the game and you hear chatter that you normally don't hear. You're not trying to listen, but it's a murmur like, "Hold up, what did you say? 'Pass the ball?' What do you mean?" They're yelling stuff at you from the stands. Now you're the target. It wasn't that I wasn't producing, but we had plenty of holes with that team.

We had a brand-new team that final year, a new coach in Fred Hoiberg. Jo and Mike Dunleavy hurt, and both miss half the season. Jimmy gets hurt. We both play about the same amount of games. Pau Gasol gets hurt. Miss the play-offs. "It's on me? What do you mean, on me?" But that was the wrong way to take it.

Normally I'm good at handling those things, but that last year I felt it change. Articles dropping in the morning paper, where a fan who goes to the game to get drunk with his friends reads it, and he's like, "Oh, he's not doing well. That's why the motherfucker's terrible, he's not doing work." Gets four beers in him. "Yeah, that's why your ass don't work, motherfucker!"

That's what was going on. I'm hearing that, looking at the people like, "Come on, you're not even here to be a fan. You're just here to fuckin' troll people." And even if they are drunk or whatever, it hurts. I was sensitive. That's the last thing I wanted to be, sensitive about it, but knowing how much I gave, it did hurt. Nobody understands how much you dedicate yourself.

But don't get me wrong, that was just at the end, and it was me who didn't handle the criticism right. There really was love for so long. I love Chicago and I still love the Bulls. That's why I ask them if I can work out there when I'm in Chicago. I don't do that other places. Stopped by to see Jerry Reinsdorf when I was there after that first season in Minnesota. Told him how much I appreciated everything he did for me. I remember after my ACL, Jerry Reinsdorf coming around to see how I was. He cared about the players. If anything, I was more hurt that I would have to leave, be away from my family and my son, PJ, being able to come to the games. Everything gonna have to change. It was an emotional time.

I LOVED THAT TEAM I CAME TO with the Bulls as a rookie. Great character guys. Don't get me wrong, all the teammates I had in Chicago were great players. Just wasn't a star at that time. Miami had the star with D-Wade. But I was lucky because the Bulls were this really good team with good guys, just had that crazy year before I was drafted—coach fired, assistant coach in, missing the playoffs for the first time in a long time. But great players.

Like Luol Deng, he's a laid-back dude. Lu was the first guy who really made me start taking care of my body. He used to do these recovery things. Even after he just had a great game—28 points, outplayed Carmelo Anthony, won the game—but then he's always doing something to help his body. Either on the bike, lifting, or doing high contrast. I didn't understand it when I was younger because I would rarely go in the training room. Used to go right past it. I'm on the court, shooting, looking for my spots.

So to see him do that made me reevaluate what I was doing as a pro. I began to think, "If I'm a pro, I've got to do it this way because he's doing it this way." Maybe if I followed Lu sooner, things would have been different. I did learn a lot about my body. It was something I learned also from my short time in Cleveland with LeBron, just how much he took care of his body. He was always doing something in the morning: lifting, basketball recovery. He's on top of everything, totally dedicated. Fifteen years in and he gets in that routine. It took me years to get my routine.

It takes some different level of dedication to do the recovery things; that's why Lu can miss a season like he did in L.A. and still come back. After the game, you wanna go out with your friends. I was going to clubs early on with the Bulls. It takes a disciplined person to say, "I'm gonna eat in the crib and put something on TV." And it's a Friday. There ain't too many people doing that. Lu was special.

That's part of the reason why I didn't think it was right to be talking about getting other guys, but I'll get to that later. Right after the injuries, the second and third with the knee, the two MCLs, that's when it started changing with my body. It all clicked at once where it was, "I've got these great examples in front of me. Lu, Jo, all of them take care of their body. I might as well."

I had to learn my body. Learning what to eat, learning how to stretch, learning how to recover. I've got a different body. I probably gotta do three or four times as much recovery as everybody else. You throw in injuries and now I gotta overdo it. Even before the surgeries, people were telling me you'll recover more than other people because your burst is quicker than a lot of people. I didn't pay no attention until I got injured. I never wanted to look at myself as being different. But in reality, I'm quicker than a lot of people. I had to take care of my body totally different than anyone else. It was a hard lesson to learn.

Now I sit in the house all the time. You see my NormaTec recovery boots plugged in, buffers everywhere. I got the whole training kit in my house. I try to get in as much recovery as possible all year, throughout the day, so the next day I'm able to go out there and not feel sluggish. When I make it to town, I go eat, get my snacks, sit in bed, turn on the movie, stretch, talk on the phone, FaceTime, but doing recovery the whole time. From when I get in until I go to sleep. In the summer, all day after I work out.

Look, nobody really wants to do that stuff. It sucks getting up in the morning and you feel like shit. Like right after the season, I take a break, a week or two off to not do anything. But my muscles tighten up right away. So imagine going a month or two months like that? Come back, muscles fatigued. You gotta wake everything back up. I jump a lot of rope, do ladder work. Just try to keep my body kind of fit so I don't have to get into shape again and again. I can gradually get into shape instead. Staying in shape, kind of. That's my life now.

I never saw Ben Gordon lift. Another great teammate. He was quiet, professional, great shooter, good guy. Every person the Bulls drafted, they were professionals, no knuckleheads. Some had some missteps along the way, but you didn't have to worry about them in the locker room like that. Those are the kinds of guys you want on your team.

I really didn't talk to Ben that much, but when we were on the floor, we had an understanding. Like in that seven-game playoff series the first year with Boston, with Ben just making big shot after big shot. That's another dawg. Somebody who is going to play the way I play.

You feed off each other. You see somebody go get three buckets in a row and you're like, "I see you, watch this." That's the way it was with me and Ben. Ben was cool, always laid-back, chill, but a dawg. He could score the ball on anyone with ease. You're getting your easy buckets at the end of the game because of him—they have to watch him. I had 36 that first playoff game in Boston.

Ben helped make it easy for me. I really wanted him to stay. I didn't understand it, why he had to leave as a free agent. But to each his own.

I don't know if it's a rumor, but you hear he wished he'd just took the money he was offered from the Bulls instead of leaving. He'd probably still be in the league right now. But he went to Detroit and there was no opportunity. You can have talent, but you need the opportunity. That's what I was fighting after I got traded to New York. With the Bulls, he could know they were still gonna use him. We needed him at the time.

THAT FIRST SEASON WITH VINNY DEL NEGRO was a little bit chaotic. I guess I was part of that with my apple-slicing injury. Someone told me it was the new meaning of slashing guard. Funny, right? But it wasn't some made-up excuse for something else that happened. I really did just roll over on a knife in bed.

I know, stupid.

I'm in the bed, Randall's upstairs. I used to buy those tough taffy apples at the time. I'm getting ready to cut this apple, and I put the knife on the bed to get the apple in my hand. Then I swing the covers upward looking for the knife, but the knife is right there and it gets me. Freak thing. I didn't tell Randall. I just left. Randall comes in and there's a pile of blood all over the bed and he said he was thinking somebody stabbed me. He said he just saw the blood and freaked.

But I knew no one was going to believe me. That became a lot of my career when it came to my name. Just had to deal with it. I understand some of my stories are bizarre. I get it.

Anyway, I called the Bulls and the trainer. I got stitched up, 10 stitches, and I practiced that same day. I know people were saying some girlfriend stabbed me or some shit like that, but I was legit just eating an apple in bed. Not smart, I know, but never in my life have I had an altercation with a girl.

The funny thing is, Randall is the most relaxed and chill dude, so I can only imagine how panicked he was when he saw it. The blood was everywhere in the bed like a horror movie. I just took the car and left.

That season we were just trying to fit together, with me and all the stuff that happened before and the new coach. But I was grateful to Vinny and the rest of the guys there. He and my teammates allowed me to play through my mistakes. That's huge when you're a rookie.

Vinny was great for me. Ben was scoring for us, Lu also. That was when we had Del Harris as an assistant. He was the first coach to curse me out. One day, he thought I was laughing in a meeting about his zone defense. He went on some long lecture like he always did about how I don't know shit and nobody knows shit—heard he told John Paxson that one time—and how he wrote six books on the zone defense and no one knows it like him.

So he curses me out—but it wasn't me laughing, it was Tyrus Thomas. Same old stuff. Gonna pick me out because I'm quiet. I think he knew it was Tyrus, but he picked me out because he knew I wouldn't say anything.

But I remember that year being cool. We were doing everything to get to the playoffs and we made it, got to that Boston series, my coming out, our coming out.

We were having a tough start, but it really changed that season when we made the trade to get John Salmons and Brad Miller. We kind of clicked right after that. John opened up the offense. He was another threat, something we needed. Everybody was trying to stop me getting to the rim. We just needed somebody else to make a few shots along with Ben. I thought we really had something there then.

I don't like to come off aggressive. Whenever I play with a team, I'm not the guy who's gonna come out and shoot 25 shots. I like working my way into that spot by getting my teammates' trust, and if you're good enough, the ball is gonna find you. In close situations, some guys don't like taking shots.

For me, I just wanted to play a solid game. It was never about taking over right away. It was like, "Alright, I got 82 games this year. I gotta find a way to get through these 82."

I always get asked about that second season with Vinny, and especially that two-handed dunk over Goran Dragic in Phoenix. The reason why I jumped that high was because I was scared he was gonna take my legs out from under me, the way he was coming from my left. Tyrus threw me the pass ahead. I wanted to have a chance to get to the rim if Dragic did try to take my legs out, to brace on the rim. When he hit me he actually lifted me up a little higher and I was able to bounce off of him and throw it in and still land. When I was younger, I used to practice dunks a lot. My first time dunking was in seventh grade, so I'd been practicing my dunks for awhile. I knew when he hit me I didn't have to hold onto the rim.

I missed just one game that first season and then came those playoffs. That experience was hard, because you had to rest. But being so young, you just want to be out in the city, especially after a game like the first one, with the way we won in Boston. Game 2, I admit, I kind of felt my legs getting a little tired. That's what they mean by the veteran thing—they know.

I got the Rookie of the Year by scoring more. But I'm not thinking about my age or thinking I'm too young. I'm thinking I'm in this league with you, so we're on the same level: NBA players. I don't care if you're older than me. That's the way I looked at it, and I think that's why I was able to do what I did in that Boston series, set the rookie scoring record or tie it, whatever.

I'm looking at that paper and I'm averaging 14 to 16 points. I look on the other side and some guy is averaging 26, 28, but we're in the same place. It's also why I said that thing about the MVP that season when Thibs came: "Why not me?" I was asked at that press conference when we were starting the season and I remember I said, "Why not?" I had been playing against these guys and doing what I did. I didn't mean it as a brag, just felt I worked as hard as anyone, I was dedicated to the game and sacrificed a lot at a young age— too much, I realized later.

I knew I could get even better and I knew these guys I was playing and how I could play against them. Plus, my team was asking me to do a lot, more than I really expected when I came into the NBA. It's always the way I approached bas- ketball. Don't back off.

Just like in life—not "Why?" but "Why not?"

I THINK A LOT ABOUT MY TEAMMATES from Chicago, like Carlos Boozer. Booz was the most energetic person I've ever been around. Day in and day out, same person, loud-loud, crazy handshakes throughout the entire day. I remember one time Fred Tedeschi, our trainer, was giving somebody a shot in the butt. Now Booz, after he used to leave the court before the game on his way back to the locker room, he used to sneak in the training room and find Fred and scare him. So this one time Fred is putting a needle in somebody's butt and Booz is sneaking up behind them, but he don't see that somebody's in front of Fred. Booz scares Fred and Fred almost breaks the needle in the guy's butt. I tell you, Fred was so fucking mad, everybody was mad. Only time I ever saw Fred get mad like that. He turned around because he couldn't believe Booz had the audacity to do it. Sure was funny.

Or like when Booz painted his head. We're in Boston and practicing and he came in the locker room and we made him take the hat off and that's when we saw it. Ooh, it looked like somebody painted that on. Man painted his head to get hair. And when the light hit it, it really shined.

That second season with Vinny, I thought we were starting to get something going. I made the All-Star team, but then almost didn't get to play after the thing with Dwight Howard where he took me out of the air in a game just before the All-Star break. Never said anything to him. I never really have relationships with guys. Other than being on the court, talking on the court. I get off the court and I live a totally different life, not an NBA life.

I remember that second season, us coming together as a team more and everything just being fun—and realizing that we probably had something here. Maybe it didn't look like it to y'all, but we had guys. And even though the Cavs beat us in five games in those playoffs, it was like, "Alright, we're not that far away. Next year we're gonna be better, closer." Just getting to the playoffs and being in games—and you're gonna lose a game, but you know you gave your all and it was just one mistake here or there that cost you the game. I think two games were decided by two points in that series. The playoffs, that's where either you're gonna die as a team or you're gonna grow as a team.

That was the series where Jo was saying those things about Cleveland and everyone was mad. It was funny stuff though. I was always closest with Jo and it was always funny to hear him talk like that. That's the New York side of him. I loved that. Like standing up, got your back, got his back. Jo's like my brother, but that stuff, with, "Who goes on vacation to Cleveland?" I had to giggle a little bit. I loved it because when you're battling like that, what do you expect? It's the NBA, grown men, not high school basketball. If you're looking to hand out trophies to everybody, watch another sport. NBA: No Boys Allowed. It's not as much like that right now, and I kind of miss that.

After that series, I kind of felt something different, like it was time for us. I didn't take much time off, just locked myself in the gym that summer doing two-a-days. Back then, I wasn't working on my body that much, it was just gym work, just torturing myself. Shooting, running layups, trying to perfect my craft. Hours and hours in the gym, just fucking with the ball. Working on my fundamentals, jab steps, getting ready. I really thought after that it proved we had a team identity.

We were coming together as a team even though we lost like that. Realizing we did probably have something going, it was, "Alright, we're really not that far away. Next year we're going to be better. We're getting that identity, growing."

You always want to play with another great player. Come on, my whole history I was helping my teammates score. I wasn't going to be surprised if I was playing with LeBron after that series, not with all the free agency stuff in that summer of 2010. Bron is a once-in-a-generation player. He's big, he knows how to use his body, he worked on his game, he worked on his shot, and he's getting more cerebral later on in his career. He's playing the game like chess now. Where he's manipulating the game and we take it for granted, kind of, that he's able to do all these things.

I'm not a "What if?" person, but if he had come to Chicago, I think we would have won the championship. I don't know how many, but I think we would have got at least one. The championship box would have been checked off and that was big for me. I would have loved to have played with Bron back then. When I was in Cleveland, it was cool playing with him. I actually went there because of him. After what happened in New York, I wanted to be somewhere I had a chance to really win again. I had some chances to go to other teams where I could maybe have played more, made more money, but I wanted to be back in that kind of place. I just hate losing.

I know my critics were saying I wouldn't want to play with LeBron, we couldn't play together, whatever. But I can play with anybody. What about him and D-Wade? They were basically two slashers and drivers, but they got it to work—two championships, Finals every season. You figure out a way. But it didn't matter. They had it planned anyway in Miami. You'd hear that season the Big Three were going to Miami before all that summer recruitment stuff.

D-Wade was always tough to play against because he knew how to get fouled. He wasn't a shooter—LeBron, neither—but it's hard playing against guys who know how to get fouled. He's gonna get you to a spot, to an angle where you think he's gonna drive, and then do something different. He's gonna step back and hit you with a pump fake to make you jump. Late in the games he was deadly. He used to change the whole game in the fourth quarter because he played that way.

The Bulls were talking to so many guys that summer, but I was cool with whoever they brought in. What was I supposed to say, "Go get me a shooter, get me D-Wade, Bron"? Nah. I like the way Derek Jeter did it. He didn't recruit—although I did make a video for the Bulls, but it was never talked about. Jeter said he'd get better, that was his job. There are so many guys in the league who would be great to play with. That's the way I felt, but I just worked on getting better.

Playing against someone like Russell Westbrook is different. Because you're playing against a freak of nature. He has a crazy amount of energy. He's going to crash every time to get a rebound. And everything is set up around him or everything is set up off the way he plays. It's hard playing against someone like that. But I for sure love it. The reason I love it is because you're kind of at a disadvantage because some guys you're not gonna stop what they do. I know people compared me and Russ because of the way we attacked the basket, but a big thing of pride for me that's always overlooked, I feel, is my court IQ. Like, I'm out there naturally playing a raw game, like Russ, but I'm also controlling the game—you gotta be paying attention.

Like the game against Golden State in Thibs' last season in Chicago. I got a quadruple double. Well, could have—I had the 11 turnovers. It was a game Jimmy didn't play. Eleven turnovers, Jimmy's out, a game we're supposed to lose. They're beating everyone in their building that season, but we got that one on a buzzer-beater. Those are games I cherish. Not so much for that last shot, but for controlling things, like a straight outdoor park game, just going at one another.

Let me tell you what I think greatness is in the league. I think greatness is guys who make a certain position special. Like when Charles Barkley came. What did he do? He pushed the ball up the floor. KG pushed the ball up the floor. What happened? Gave them the freedom to move about the floor. Just like any point guard would want. Like Bob Cousy dribbling up the floor. But then they got systematic during the '80s and '90s. AI came and look what happened. He was a pioneer. That's a little bit more freedom. Now there's guys like James Harden. Tough playing defense on him because of his moves. He knows how to get fouled, too, like D-Wade, and people overlook how strong he is. He'll make it look kind of simple, but it's different if you're out there playing against him. He brings a level of strength that's rare at that position. Anthony Davis is unique because he has that motor. He can change the game on the defensive side of the floor, too. Dwight, he could run the floor at a time most bigs were slow. Dwight was just an action figure.

There's levels of players, but it's different when you see them as a player does, when you play against them. Fans and media don't always see the whole game the way the player looks at it. Every player I ever played against at my position, they're great—that's why they're in the league. They're great players and it's my job to make it hard on them when I play them. That's always the way I looked at it, that when you play me you know it's gonna be a hard game. It's not gonna be a walkover game. No matter what game I was in. Not like it's me against you or some battle with talking going on. Just make it hard. If I played bad, then next game I'm gonna go out and play harder. That was always the way I did it.

I DID THE LeBRON RECRUITING FOR CHICAGO. It was a day after practice, and Bron and Chris Bosh and all of them, we got word—everyone heard it around the league—they were together on one of those banana boat things and were about to team up somewhere. Gar Forman, our GM, came to me with the people from the office about putting a video together for Chris Bosh, D-Wade, and Bron. I didn't fight it. I did the video. I'm sure Bron and those guys saw it. Then this story came out that I wasn't big on recruiting. Should I have to say that I recruited? That's where I'm coming from. It's a lose-lose. I'm not comfortable saying I'm out there recruiting because I respect my teammates. Should players have to do that? It doesn't seem right.

When I saw the story was "Derrick doesn't want to recruit," I felt like, as my partner in this, the Bulls should have come out and said I'd done it. Like, "We got it. Chill. He cool."

They didn't.

But I'm the type of guy where whatever you're saying about me, as long as I'm on the court, I don't care. I'll take the hit. I was immature at the time and I didn't want to say that I did a video because I felt that they were supposed to say stuff like that for me. Maybe they agreed with that story though? Maybe they wanted me to do more? I can understand that, too, but I was doing my stuff.

I didn't care who I played with. I feel like I'm just gonna try to get the job done. No matter who is on the floor with me, play the way you can play. You'd think that's what everyone would want from a player, to give it his all no matter who he's playing with. That's the weird thing with all the teaming up guys have done. I'm glad the players have their rights and we can make decisions for our families, but I also like the challenge of showing you what we can do as a team no matter who we've got.

That's how we felt with Thibs and the Bulls when we had the best record in the league. I feel like as a player my job is to show I'm progressing every year. You see I'm progressing every year, so in my mind I'm showing you—that's the real recruiting. That's who players should want to be with. The way I felt was, "I'll show you that I'm getting better every year, that I'm holding up my half." Then it's up to them.

I never came into it in a way where I started the conversation of getting a free agent, saying you gotta get better players, get this guy, get that guy. *I* had to get better. It was on me. But there was always someone asking me about what the Bulls should do in free agency. I never came out and said, "This is what I wanna do about free agency." It was always me being asked. If I wasn't asked, we would've never talked about it. I would've just waited like with anything else, until they got someone. They got Booz, Kyle Korver, C.J. Watson, Kurt Thomas—I liked our team.

And then we got Thibs.

WHEN TOM THIBODEAU GOT IN, that's the first time I'd seen a coach hold players accountable the way he did. He just doesn't let up. As a player like myself who doesn't say much—everyone always wanted me talking, that leader stuff, but like this book, I'm someone who is gonna show you—I appreciated it because it keeps me on point. I don't need anybody on me like a micromanager, but I respect it because he makes it seem like he loves the game more than you.

The funny thing about that is he wouldn't have to say shit. It was you coming in and he's there at 5:30 in the morning. Like, "What the fuck are you doing?" Or you have practice, you go home, then you're like, "I'm going to take some guys over here and shoot." So you go in and it's like 9:00 PM and he's still there. Y'all got a game the next day. Like, "What you doing here? We had practice like seven hours ago." He brought structure to the team.

You could have an open relationship with him. We talked about everything. He could tell me everything. It was always basketball. He never hid nothing from me about basketball. I just remember it being a hell of a year. I remember smiling a lot. Everybody was enjoying being on the road. That season was one of those things that I'll cherish, one of those years where you're number one. You know how it is in the league when you're having a season like that. You're gonna get fans following you everywhere. All that type of stuff. You become more of an act instead of a team. It was cool, and we played good basketball.

We won 62 games that first year, the most in the league, and beat Miami all three times we played them in the regular season. Fun playoff games, too. Each one close, tough, right down to the end, held the scores down in the 80s, 90s. LeBron didn't play in that first regular season game, but D-Wade was great. Me and D-Wade in the last two minutes, back and forth. Kyle made a big shot and we won. Then it was Lu the next time we played them—big shot, after we were down again. Then beat them that third time when I made a few shots at the end. See, I used to be able to shoot. Ha! Were just trying to win games. Fun games. Things seemed to be going right. No problems, and I only missed one game that season, with, I think, a stiff neck.

I loved it. Not only were we good, we were also cool enough that we could have a dialogue with one another: "Alright, you missed me on my guy driving to the hole. That was supposed to be a floppy. Next time, be there." Jo, he's gonna come out and curse me and tell me. Or Lu was gonna curse me and tell me. Joakim or myself or anybody could talk to Thibs that way. I think that made us close as a team, because in the heat of the moment somebody could get emotional and it was okay. A real team, you know what I mean?

It'll throw you off when the person gets emotional out of nowhere. With us, we might have that moment and then it's, "Okay, what's the play now? That's over. We can talk about this after the game." We calmed it down. "This is the play we're doing. We're trapping him on this." When we were out there, Thibs was the one holding everyone accountable. You didn't have to go and talk to someone else crazy like that.

We used to party together. That was the team when everybody was together. We had arguments a few times in the locker room, but we knew what was important to the team. Fans and media don't realize how much that goes on, but if you're a team and respect one another, it's good. Sometimes it could be the littlest things. Thibs would be mad at Jo for breaking a play or forgetting the play. Jo actually did that a lot. Jo would break the play and then do something better. It would be a plus. But Thibs, he's controlling. So he would be on Jo even though things worked out better, like, "What the fuck are you doing!"

And Jo would be like, "Fuck you!"

And Thibs would be like, "No, fuck you."

No joke, they used to argue like that. But nobody overreacted. We knew they just needed to vent, get it out of their system. They were professional enough to do that and then keep going over the game plan.

One reason I think a lot of good things ended up happening with me then, like getting the MVP and all that, was that I knew the ball was going to come back to me at some point during the game. I was ready for it. We had Keith Bogans. It was rare to see him shoot two times in a row, and he wasn't viewed as a shooter. I never thought about teammates that way. I was too young to think about Keith Bogans and how everybody else viewed him in the league or the analysts at that time. I remember saying, "Keith, you're supposed to be a shooter, shoot the ball!"

That's how I looked at anyone on the team. I don't care who you are. If I put you in the position where you're open, I want you to shoot and shoot with confidence. And that's why you saw teammates of mine shoot with confidence. They could miss a majority, but they had that confidence. They flourished off that. The main thing for me was Thibs allowing me to play freely. He was running the offense through me. I didn't have to force myself on the team. Guys go to different teams and say, "I'm such and such from that team and I shot 25 times over there. So you know what's gonna happen over here." I was never that guy. I always felt like I had to get my teammates shots.

The ball will find you, I've always believed that. And in tough games, it'll find you pretty quick. The fact that guys are scared to shoot? In the playoffs, you see that at the end of the game. Certain guys are like, "Damn, don't throw it to me!" Why did I shoot four times in a row? Because nobody on the team wants to shoot.

All of Thibs' groups were great groups, really. Everybody connected with one another. We pushed one another in practice. But we were just young toward the end there. Needed more veterans on the team. Then by that time, Thibs was mad that he wasn't getting the players that he wanted and it kind of messed up the mood of the team. And then the media kept coming at me talking about it. But I was like, "I don't have nothing to do with that. Y'all have something you want to ask them, please ask them." I wish they would have come to an understanding, Thibs and management, but they never did.

WE DID THINK WE COULD HAVE WON that season, 2010. I remember the Indiana series to start the playoffs. That really was the first series I was nervous. I wasn't really nervous for that Boston series when I was a rookie, I guess because that was my first one and, it may sound crazy, but no one gave us much chance. This time it was the big stage. For real. We were on top. It was more like a stage I hadn't been on, even with the big games I'd played in high school and college.

I think I did well, but before every game I really do remember being nervous and anxious. I think most of the time guys are, but once you start playing it's gone. Such a buildup and so many days before the series and after the end of the season. I remember Jeff Foster trying to kill me every time I went to the hole. It was physical. That's when the league was kind of trying to change that stuff. It was still physical and it was cool. I liked that kind of play. It made me focus even more. Because I'm trying to irritate the other team, trying to make them even more mad. No matter what you're doing, I'm still killing you. No matter what you're doing, I want you to feel every play. You're taking cheap shots, being dirty. Nothin'. We're still bringing it.

I think that's what really comes from playing in Chicago, being in that environment, being in that culture where you have someone at your mercy. You have to kill 'em, or they'll get you. Grew up playin' that way. Any chance that you get to destroy someone you have to take it. That's what makes a guy like Kobe, Kobe. Also getting ready to play someone like Bron and D-Wade.

I felt like we were still growing. We beat Atlanta and then the one everyone was waiting for: Chicago vs. Miami. Great series and we're down 2–1 and I had a chance at the end to win Game 4. Missed and we lost in overtime. We held them to the low 90s like we wanted, just wasn't enough.

Whenever I get shots like that, last shots, I try to clear my mind. Of course, I don't hit every one of them, but I feel like

I always learn from the ones I missed. Like, "Damn, I shot two of those shots and they went left. So why am I shooting left when it's the last seconds?" Then, "Alright, when I do my drills whenever I'm working out, I'll count down 3…2…1 on the last shot of all my drills." Just so it gets me ready to knock down those shots when I'm in the moment.

When I was younger, I used to hold on to it, and it kind of handicapped me a little because I worried about the last shot, about whether or not I should take it. It happened a few times where I didn't know whether to take the shot or not because I was missing them so much early on in my career with the Bulls. So just working on it in the gym. Counting down like a shot clock. When I catch the ball, it's a shot clock. Over and over.

By Game 4 with Miami, I was used to it. Didn't hesitate. Missed and then had one more chance and they put LeBron on me. It's tough when you have a guy that size, but like I said, I was wishing they'd do that the whole game. They didn't. I missed, but I had to put it behind me right away. I couldn't think about it like that. Especially knowing there's still overtime left. It was just a play to me: I didn't execute, but there's another one coming.

I know people might laugh now and say it's an excuse and we're crazy, but ask anyone on that team—Lu, Taj Gibson, Thibs—and they'll tell you: losing Omer Asik was big. Miami had a problem when we had him paired with Jo and Kurt Thomas. We could play them tougher, and Omer really had verticality that gave them trouble. He got hurt in the third game and that was huge. Played every game that season until then and then he's out. Again, injuries. We really were closer than anyone believed. And they knew it. We felt they knew we were the team they weren't going to intimidate.

Every game that we played against them under Thibs was like that, intense and challenging. You know how playoffs are? Whoever makes the right adjustments, that's who's gonna win. And they made the right adjustments. The turnovers—I think I had like seven or eight—were just from overthinking, trying to get us over. I knew I had to score for us to stay in the game. But it was okay. They were trying to make me exhausted out there on the defensive end so I wouldn't have energy to attack them on the offensive end.

Then we think we have Game 5 won and they came back quick and just like that, it's over. We're thinking we've got that, we're going back to Miami and…what did they score, like 14 points in two minutes? D-Wade makes a four-point play and they're going to the Finals. That's what hurt most. Being up that many points and thinking we had a grip on the game and they just made the plays. We were supposed to be that team.

It did teach me something else, too. That's when me and BJ started talking about how to finish games in the league. Like, it's okay for a team you're playing against to be up like that. Sometimes you don't mind at all if a team is up 10 on you in the fourth quarter, because then they play a totally different game. Then when you get close they tighten up and lose the game. When he said it to me, I knew exactly what he was talking about. And I was able to affect the game in that way. "Alright, we're down 14, 16, it's gonna be tough. Let's get it to eight with four minutes left." Sort of like a horse race where a horse gets tired leading all the way, and if you're behind you can make a run. That's how I was going to be looking at it, feeling we would finish games better. Just didn't know how yet because we were so young. We were getting ready.

And then came the injury.

YEAH, THE ACL, IT WAS LIFE CHANGING. Right away after the ACL in April 2012, I was emotional in the hospital because basketball was over with. For the time being, anyway. It was done and I thought we were so close the way that season went. But now I had to wrap my mind around the rehab. A long rehab—and I hate rehab. It's lonely and hard.

I had to wear a brace for the first four months, had to sleep with it the first three months. You can't sleep, you can't roll over. With your partner, you gotta watch whoever's in the bed. You have to really watch everything around you. I became an expert at it, though, something you don't want. I asked the doctors right away, "How many times a week do I have to go?" And it was just like I was afraid it would be. Every rehab session I did, I was miserable.

But I did it because with the proper rehab you kind of bounce back to how you were. I believed that.

So, you start with weight lifting, which starts at 8:00, 8:30 in the morning. Every day, first thing, head to the facility. Get stretched on the table, mold the scar tissue, do the flexibility, take measurements of your flexibility. Then you start off by getting on the bike to warm up your knee, then start running and pounding. The bike is for circulation. You can walk on the treadmill for five or 10 minutes. Either way, once you get off the bike or the treadmill, you do the deceleration drills, then acceleration drills, which is kind of like a track-and-field workout.

Deceleration is the hardest part of coming back from an ACL. Every doctor will tell you that. You've got no balance. You don't have confidence in your joints. It takes a lot of repetition. Running, that's fine. That's what people watching me never understood. I could run—it wasn't about that. Even then you've got to build your muscles back up, build everything back up.

I'd always played basketball all summer and then into the season. Now, from 8:00 in the morning until, shit, I mean, until after the game once the season started, it's just rehab.

Work out before the games. Go back there, put the ice on. Do all the recovery stuff. Every day. They have you talk to different therapists. All of them are the same. They just try to get you to vent to them and see what's going on, the mental stuff. But I felt like I could've easily gotten over it myself by getting healthy. I didn't feel like I had to talk to anyone. I was only sad because I wasn't healthy. I felt like if I just got healthy everything would be alright. I shut down when it's like that. Stay to myself. Most of the time I just watch a lot of documentaries. And then I'll work out as soon as I can.

In the summer, it's rehab first. Then I did basketball after my rehab. Two-a-days. I needed to make sure all the muscles were on the same wavelength or pattern or whatever because if one of your muscles is buried, that's gonna cause overcompensating, just like it did later when I tore my MCL.

Like, oh shit! It just came out of nowhere. A flap just opened up, just a little clip. A lot of it is because of the way my body is. I get bulky real quick. That's just my body type. I'm big, strong for a point guard. I'm still fast even though my knees are not the same. Somehow my body's overcompensating to play the way I want to play. But with a lot of guys they're not able to do that because they're not that type of athlete. When you are, though, I found out it can cause different problems.

WITH ME, I THINK ONE REASON there was so much controversy was because of Adrian Peterson, the football player. He comes back from his ACL after what, eight or nine months? He played football, so everything's totally different, but I don't know how anybody does that naturally. That's why I was saying, "Come on, man. The same year?" When I came back in early 2013, those last months around the team I was working out, shooting, but I wasn't able to move around the way I normally did. So I know it wasn't right.

You're getting advice from everyone. The doctors are who the doctors are—they're *team* doctors. They say you're fine. But when you run into players, they ask about your injuries, and they're like, "Take a year. That shit normally takes at least a year." Everyone's telling me that. I wanted to come back sooner, but my body was telling me, "No, wait a little bit." My knees were still sore. My stuff isn't supposed to feel this way. That's why I took longer, because I felt my body wouldn't hold up. But the media didn't want to hear that.

For me, all I was thinking about was redemption, just trying to get it back. The first time you're hurt you have trouble believing it happened. It's, "No, I can deal with this. I handle everything." But in reality, my body, the ACL, it was taking longer. And that's what I was fighting the whole time. I wanted to be back faster, but that's when I learned about listening to your body. I was doing too much, working out too much. I wanted to feel like I could prep myself for whatever. I didn't want any excuses. I felt like I can always work out. If I put my mind to it, I could get it done. Like I always did. If I'm in my regular workout routine during the season and I have a bad game or something, I blame it on that workout I didn't do. I didn't do the preparation, and that's on me. So I took that mentality into the ACL rehab, that I would do everything and get back sooner. But I was really doing too much and not letting it happen more naturally.

Holding my Rookie of the Year award with Reggie, my mom, and Dwayne.
(AP Images)

When I was younger, I used to practice dunks a lot. On Goran Dragic in 2010. (Mark J. Rebilas–USA TODAY Sports)

Jo, Luol, me, and Booz in 2010. I liked our team. (AP Images)

Someone asked what my expectations were for myself going into my third year. I said, "Why can't I be the MVP of the league?" (Mike DiNovo-USA TODAY Sports)

I didn't know President Obama was a big Bulls fan until I met him in person.
(Newscom/Official White House Photo by Pete Souza)

I fixed the rims and the court at Murray Park, right around the corner from our place on Paulina. I try to help quietly. (AP Images)

Even if we had a better regular season, LeBron would stop us every time in the playoffs. (AP Images)

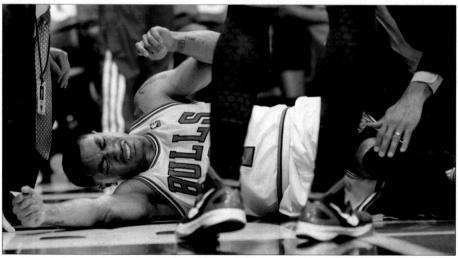

Yeah, the ACL, it was life changing. (AP Images)

Because I wasn't someone who talked much, I think that made wearing the "I Can't Breathe" T-shirt louder. (Newscom/Chris Sweda-Chicago Tribune)

A lot of people don't understand the connection I have with Thibs. There's this communication I have with Thibs that's different. (AP Images)

By that last year in Chicago, we started losing and things were getting away. But I was still emotional when I heard about the trade to the Knicks. (AP Images)

Whenever I'm in China, I feel the love. (AP Images)

I really thought we were going to have a special team in New York. But when it came to the basketball, I knew right away that we were shit. (AP Images)

Having my kids has played a huge role in understanding where I am and where I will be.

(Instagram @laylamaliburose)

A 50-point night and a blocked shot to win the game on Halloween in 2019. Like, out of all the bullshit I went through, all the adversity I went through, it was my way of showing myself that I still have it. (AP Images)

I've been that way my whole career. My back was against the wall already, even more when people started doubting me. I was like, "Hold up! I'll work out even more then." But the funny thing is, throughout that entire time I didn't have any jealousy about other guys in the league. I never felt jealous of my peers for what I was going through and seeing them do what they did, passing me by like they were. What that really did was push me to go harder in my workouts. Like, "Damn, Russ had a good year. I gotta go hard. Steph just had two good years! I gotta go even harder." You know what I mean? Some people are jealous of other people's success. But I know that shit can tear you down. I didn't want to bring the negative energy. You've got to use that as more motivation in your life.

I don't want this to sound like I'm boasting or something, but with a hooper it's like being an artist. Not your typical artist like most people think of, like a dancer or rapper or painter, but an artist. That's how I feel—how we feel as hoopers. I was not gonna go out there and show you a half of me, give you a bullshit performance and then it's on me and I can't sleep because I'm letting you down. Like me missing the free throw at the end of the game or me not performing and not giving you the oohs and ahhs at the end of the game. What's the point of my playing then?

If I go out there and you see that night that I played with my knee not right—and forget what it means for my future, which is a lot—everyone'll still be critiquing my game, saying maybe I let the team down, maybe I was selfish and I shouldn't have played. Is a singer going to go out there with their voice croaking and hurt? No. You owe it to your fans to give them the best performance. I couldn't do that and I knew that. If I don't take the year off, I don't think I have any career after that. But what am I giving you if I do come back too soon? It didn't make any sense.

Of course, my critics weren't saying that.

I knew pretty soon I wasn't coming back that year. My knee wasn't ready, not close. I had the surgery in May 2012. Everyone says a year, and now you look around at more guys who have had it, like Rajon Rondo, Zach LaVine, Danilo Gallinari, Jabari Parker, all about a year or even more.

What they were quick to forget was what Dr. Cole said right after my surgery. He's one of the best in the world and he tells the media, "While he will hopefully be at a very high level in 12 months, it still may take slightly longer... It depends on the muscle psychology, confidence issues." He was saying 12 months from May, and probably longer.

So then in March and April I'm not playing, and something is wrong with that? How does that happen? I think one time when they were pushing me, I said, "Nobody knows but God," to say, "Come on, I'm trying." So they get mad at that? How does that happen? It's God.

Really, it's the second year after the surgery before you see most guys are close to playing like they did. You see when they come back after only about a year they're not performing at the old level yet. Zach LaVine's a good one. Look at how he was playing a year after his surgery in his first season with the Bulls. Couldn't even finish the season, because of tendinitis. Then look at the next season. He was great.

But my critics were saying I should come back in nine, 10, 11 months. Not only would that be early, that would be right at the time the playoffs started. And you know that's not regular basketball. How is that happening in my hometown? So, I withdrew. It's hard not to. I was able to move around and play—I *looked* like I was good. But I was thinking the game instead of reacting. A lot of people can think the game, but I'm a reactive player. Your body isn't ready to react like that, and not the way I play.

But I had to go along and play the game like I was coming back. Imagine if I would have said, "No, I'm not coming back." It would have been just like what Kawhi Leonard was going through that last season with the Spurs. They didn't believe him, said he was faking. Guy is injured and trying to get back, but you know you can't. "He looks okay. Where is he?" Imagine me in Chicago. "What, you ain't trying to play?" So I got on the court and I was giving them the, "Oh, I just don't feel right." In reality, my knee wasn't ready at all.

During the rehabilitation, I asked a lot of questions. They're telling me it's going to be maybe a year. I have to sleep in a boot three months, but after three months I'm thinking I should be fine. I'm thinking, "Man, you gotta get your rhythm, you gotta do all this." But I wasn't going to be able to play in the playoffs. If I'm out there not playing the way I play, it's like, "Oh, what's with him?" Probably would have traded me then. Ha!

Like, okay, that shit's over right now. They said I was cleared to play. Which doesn't mean I'm ready to play in games. I told them I wasn't ready to play. My knee was still sore after certain things, after a lot of workouts. I know I'm not ready to play, period. My whole thing came from me reacting. I'm not reacting to things I always reacted to. I know it's not right. But I'm out there pushing, trying.

I felt like when the media came into the gym in practice I had to be on the court acting like I'm working out, so I put the image out there that maybe I can play. I never went to the arena and said I don't want to play tonight. Never in my life.

Then there was the thing with my brother giving this interview. Everyone's acting like I could be playing any day now because it's maybe nine months after surgery, but my knee's not right at all. Reggie said some stuff like, "Why should Derrick come back? Y'all didn't make any trades to help the team be ready for the playoffs."

Look, you know how it is with your family. You talk about shit—everyone does. But I can't roll against my family. That shit, yeah, we talked about it. I know where that came from. He didn't have to say it in an interview though. Was he frustrated at the time? Sure. Seeing me like that, he was pissed and he expressed it in that interview. Knowing him, yeah, that's what he would do. But I'm always riding with him no matter what. That's my bro.

I couldn't believe I missed a whole season—first time I went so long without basketball since I was maybe five or six—but it was just to keep getting stronger, trying to get back, trying not to think about the knee and the surgery. I've always been someone who looks forward and I really wanted to play, but something wasn't right. You know how you have that feeling and everyone is saying everything is fine, but you just know it's not? I felt something. So I really wasn't that surprised when I hurt my knee again in Portland in November of that next season, after the one I missed.

THERE WAS SO MUCH MEDIA when I got back for the 2013 season: "What's he going to do? Can he walk?" I felt sometimes like I was in a cage and everyone was just staring at me. "Is he limping? Is he really here now?" I was playing okay, missed one game with my hamstring a little sore. I felt like I was making shots, made I think five or six three-pointers one game, getting to the rim, but my body wasn't balanced. I was super strong from taking all that time off. And I'm working all that time—I can't play, so I'm training, lifting—and when my body is like that, when I get too strong, it throws things off. If I'm not balanced, that's when things really get bad. My hips are not aligned. I found out that's when I really get in the risk area.

I know that now, but I really didn't know that then. I just felt…not right. A little scared about that, too. But after being away so long, I felt that was just natural, that you feel like that. I didn't know my body then like I do now. I was lifting both my legs up, lifting my upper body up. I was way overweight. At least 215, big for no reason. But that's what happens when you can't play. You figure you'll get stronger, be in better condition, that it'll help you.

But it was too much pressure on my knees. I was pushing myself to get back, probably pushed too much. I probably should have slowed down some of my workouts, but I was so into a routine already. Couldn't wait to be back. Once I get in a routine, it's like most people trying to get out of it. I felt like I was too far in and I feel that's what led up to my other knee injuries.

It was hard when that happened in Portland. Just a simple back cut. I was having my best game yet that season. I think I had just made a three early in the third quarter and that gave me 20 points. We were having a good game in a place that was always tough to play. Funny, we always were winning when shit happened. Then just a cut to the basket, but even though I knew something was wrong right away, I also knew I had a chance of playing again.

Just like after my ACL, I kept saying to myself, "As long as it's not an ACL." That's how I coped this time. "Any injury, I injure whatever, as long as it's not the ACL." I never want to go through that again. You really have to learn how to walk and run again. I knew I was gonna play again, but I didn't know if I was gonna have that burst of speed because of this being a knee again. Or if I was gonna have enough confidence to play the way I wanted to play without thinking. That's the big mental thing with the injuries, and for me the mental has been a big part. It's not all about, "Can I play like that and have my speed?" It's about having to go through this again, the rehab. It was gonna be another long winter, but I knew I was going to play again.

Actually, it was going with the USA team that began to change everything. My hair, too. Time to become Samson?

IT WAS ONLY LATER THAT I REALIZED I had been pushing my body too far.

My body is different than everybody else's. You don't think of that kind of thing when you're young, just playing, and especially having success like I did. Because everything seems so natural and right. My body bulks up real quick. What I was doing was throwing my body out of whack because I wasn't letting my legs adjust naturally. It took me years to learn that. I was making one leg stronger than the other. Then the next rehab, I'm making my left leg stronger than my right. I was getting too much force in one leg. I always felt off balance. But when you hurt your knee like that you don't really know what's normal and what's not, because you never went through it, and then people are telling you all kinds of things. It's tough. You're going through all this stuff yourself and wondering and questioning, and then all anybody wants to know is when you are gonna play and if you'll be what you used to be.

It was with my last run with the USA team in 2014 at the World Championships that I finally put everything together. It got to, "I'm gonna train different, slow down on the weight lifting. I have to lose my weight." The weight irritated me and really was hurting me. You have to go through these kinds of things to understand. You're told so many different things and you have to make decisions for yourself, even if you're not the doctor. How do you know?

I finally stumbled on it in New York in summer 2014. I was seeing doctors there. We saw a doctor when we were overseas. Nobody could explain why my knee was sore until I got back and the season was starting. I changed the way I ate a little bit, started losing weight, and so my knee had less of a load on it.

I was glad I played for USA Basketball, appreciated Mike Krzyzewski and Jerry Colangelo picking me. I know some people thought I was upset that year because I was coming off the bench. But I didn't really care. What was really crazy about that whole situation is that I heard the conversation about me not being a starter—I actually overheard Coach K and Colangelo talking about it, but I wasn't trying to. They hadn't said anything to me about starting Kyrie, but then I overheard them talking about it.

We were somewhere out of the country and I was going upstairs to get a massage. While I'm getting a massage, I hear two men talking. You know, overseas the walls are so thin you can hear everything. So I hear them talking about Kyrie, talking about the future of the team, and the direction they were going with the team. It was actually cool to hear. They didn't say anything bad about me. Just saying that they felt it was a good decision to go with starting him, the rotations that they had. What blew my mind about it was that they were out in public talking about that. And there I was in the next room over. They started me some games, started him some games. They just were saying, "We like Kyrie in that spot." I wasn't upset or disappointed. Whatever was best for the team to win. It was just, I was hearing it, like, "Damn, can't you take your conversation in private?"

The other funny thing about being with that USA team— it's not so funny, actually—is that with the way basketball is these days, with sponsors especially, it's like you're either in or out. You really have to be with their sponsors, with ESPN, with Nike, like Bron. Not that Bron isn't great, but it's also why you always see Bron on TV. If you're not with them, like I was with Adidas, it's different. It's all, "Sorry, just the way it is." The big picture for the NBA is ESPN and Nike. For instance, when I was playing for that USA team, my brother tried to go up there and get an iPad from Nike because they were having them for the players. But they told him, "No, we don't got no iPad for an Adidas guy."

I'm on the team. But because I'm Adidas, I don't get no iPad?

I remember, I was like, "Reg, can you go get my iPad?" And they were just like, "No, not for you."

That's the political part of the game. I felt that a lot after my injuries, that there was this sense of, "Just retire and be over with. You have money." Maybe people are just tired of talking about me. But when I do shit, they're all over it.

I always felt like I was still relevant, and thanks to Thibs for giving me a chance to show it with Minnesota. It's just that I have a quieter fanbase now.

In China, my fanbase is still huge. You hear all the stuff sometimes about Adidas and if I'm a problem for them, but believe me, they made their money back on me. I feel like I really had to work to get where I am, as far as a shoe deal. I wasn't handed a shoe when I made it to the league. But my stuff is huge in China and I'm still going there. That's where my sneaker money is. I may be quiet, but I know the numbers. That's why Adidas still has three active sneakers: James Harden, Damian Lillard, and mine. The D Rose 9 came out just before I went to China in August 2018. Now Adidas is talking about retros and my 10th shoe.

Family is important to people in China, and I think that's one reason why we can relate to one another. They see how me and my family are one. When you go over there, the culture is kind of the same way. Whenever I'm in China, I feel the love. I love going there—I feel that vibe. They made that video for me back in 2017, with all these fans in China saying,

"I love you, Rose." It was pretty amazing. I was emotional. It's all been a blessing.

THAT TIME WITH USA BASKETBALL was when a lot of things started to change for me. To tell you the truth, at first I thought all my injuries were just bad luck, bad karma. Until I grew my hair. That was the beginning, and things started to change.

A lot of people don't understand, but I feel with black people, our hair is everything. Our hair is power, really. That's one of the reasons that I grew my hair out again. The bad shit I was going through at that time, I began thinking that my mindset was different. It was all about revenge before. I was mad, mad at what they were saying and writing, getting in a corner. That's not who I was as a person.

After I started growing my hair back, it was like that weight was lifted off me and I could think more clearly. I know it sounds crazy, but it's real to me. Maybe people won't believe that, but that's why I look the way I do now. It's part of me being in a better place.

You can almost look at the different phases of my career through my hair. First, the short hair D-Rose, kind of like the Samson story from the Bible. I'm not religious, but with black people, our hair grows different—it's important. We're able to grow the 'fro. Our hair grows up. A lot of people's hair, if it gets too long it falls. Ours continues to grow. In other places—tribes—they used to do their hairdos up in different ways for different types of operations, occasions, different powers. The batch of hair I've got now, it totally changed me into a different person. Growing my hair out, it felt like I was gaining my strength, but also becoming more mature, more understanding, more considerate. When you're chasing greatness, it's kind of hard being right sometimes.

When the hair thing was going on, I began to leave that revenge side behind. When I first came back from my injuries, I wouldn't say I was in a dark place, but my mindset was trying to prove them wrong instead of just being me. I didn't know who I was then. It wasn't me. Now I feel like I know who I am. I know how gifted I am. I know I'm going to do great things again. So why force it? I felt like I was back then—not forcing it, just letting it organically come to me. It seemed to rejuvenate me, where all the old thoughts, I was finally able to step away from a lot of the things that'd been on me. I knew I wanted to keep my hair and I knew things would be lining up right in my life.

I FEEL LIKE THINGS ARE RIGHT WITH ME. I just love being a dad. That's the best thing for me. I always wanted to have kids and have kids early in life. I know in the NBA a lot of guys don't want kids, they want to have *that* life. And that's cool, but it's not for me. I was always in a household around kids, around infants and babies all the time, having to take care of kids for my mom and brothers and aunts and uncles. I always loved that.

When my brothers were having kids, they wanted their kids to interact with other kids too, which is important. That was my life growing up. Sure, it was tough with not so much space in the house, but you always had someone around to play with, to watch your back, someone you knew cared about you.

It was cool to see my brothers' kids. Made me feel like, "Damn, we're missing out." Feeling like I'm wanting to make our family bigger. I always saw myself having three kids. PJ, he loves kids and he needed a sibling around this time. So I'm glad he's got his sister, Layla. She's perfect because she's funny and she's just a busybody, always moving around, so it seems like she's always going to have the same energy.

Mieka Blackman Reese, she's PJ's mom. We get along great, great friends. All my stuff is relationships with my friends, me making sure everybody's on the same page. Look, I have kids with two different women. So it's on me. I'm the one who has to make sure their relationship is good, which it is. It's about communicating, having patience, caring. It ain't like my ex left me. I left her with a kid. So that's what I have to tell my girl now: "You gotta understand, she's hurting. I left her. You've gotta deal with the emotions and everything." But we're good.

PJ lives with her. But when I'm in L.A. in the summer, I'll rent a house for her just down the street from me and

PJ can stay there, stay with me. That was the toughest thing about leaving Chicago. Not being so close to him. But that's also why New York and Cleveland were good, close, could come in any time.

I met Mieka when I first made it to the league. She's from Chicago, but when I met her she was a student at Clark in Atlanta. I actually met her in Chicago, but she was going back to school in Atlanta. We dated for a long time. We were together from when I was like 19 or 20 and we didn't have PJ until I was like 24, 25. After she had PJ, we became more friends. It wasn't easy, and I was the one leaving. The relationship was stressful for both of us. So we finally agreed to just be friends. In reality, we were friends even before we were in a deep relationship. I really think of her as my friend. Just have a great relationship now. Not a document for custody. Just trust.

My daughter, Layla, was born March 4, 2018. Her mom's name is Alaina Anderson. I met her through a mutual friend and she's from Chicago. She's younger than me, about six years.

Now, PJ was named that because of Pooh Junior, but Alaina gave Layla her name. We agreed that if it was a boy, I would name him, and if it was a girl, she would name her.

Then in 2019, we had my second son, London. I feel blessed.

I DON'T REALLY HAVE RELATIONSHIPS WITH NBA GUYS, other than on the court. When I get off the court, I live a totally different life, especially now. Sure, when I was younger I used to go to the clubs, but still not with the NBA guys. They're good guys and I always got along with everyone, but it's not my kind of life. Always wanted to be with my friends, like Randall, or family. Alaina travels with me a lot now.

I wasn't sure certain times about still playing. That was true in New York that time, in Cleveland. But I was being self-ish. I had money, security—but my money is for the foundation I want to set up when I'm done playing. I've done stuff: After School Matters in Chicago, Rose Scholars, funerals I've paid for, Murray Park. But I really want to get into some serious stuff—business stuff—after I'm finished playing. It's always about giving back. I haven't gotten into it enough yet because I want to when I can be involved full time. Now, it still has to be basketball. But I really want to be able to help kids. Kids are everything with me. I feel life is about giving.

I spend what I spend, but my money is for my kids. I know I want them to be alright. I'm setting up trusts. Also prepping them to be into it, like getting used to handling the money. But I love the fact I can give my son name-brand clothes and he don't give a crap about it at all. Everybody else, of course, tells him what he's got. I love the fact he doesn't care. He's just a regular kid. I'm just so happy no one will have to worry like we did. That's what I love about my family. They're not into the things I'm into. Like I said, I'm actually into materialistic things, even though I don't show it a lot. They know clothes from me giving them gifts. They'll say, "That's nice, but I still want the $25 shirt from, you know, Target."

What my brother Reggie did was put me in position to have control over my own life. When I was younger, they used to get mad, say your brother seems so controlling. I've been this way ever since I was born, same way. Only thing changed? I got smarter. That's what kills me about it. My brothers know on any position, on anything, I always voice my opinion. I express how I feel, what I want to do. Always did. I try to do it in a respectful way, but it's me. I always felt that independence. Chicago makes you learn that to survive.

I always believe in and trust in people, but I also can tell about people when I deal with them. My financial advisor, I met her and we clicked right away. She's more like my auntie now. I trusted her to find me the private banks. I only invest my money in my trust funds—three-year options, five-year options—where you can take some risks but you're mostly being conservative.

I've got a grip on how to do this now, but at first she was making me go to all the financial meetings with the bankers to understand what was going on. I didn't know about equities, bonds, stuff like that. I studied, I learned, read about it, watched videos, went to three-hour meetings. I'm listening to these people talk. Then I started getting more money, and I'll admit I got mad about how much taxes I had to pay. That's how I also got more interested in having life insurance, a will, the different financial instruments you need to be diversified. Figuring out everything so if anything happened to me, I'm gonna have my stuff where it goes directly to my kids.

I'm not making these risky investments, like real estate and stuff I don't know about—or with people I don't know. I don't invest like that. I always felt if I wanted to invest in something—and I will eventually—I want to make Magic Johnson–type deals. His deals can change your life. I don't just want to make money. I want to make something that's gonna change people's lives and affect the community. I'm not doing a lot of that yet. I could easily throw my name on something right now. Or start something. But I don't want to. That's why I haven't started the foundation yet. I want to be able to come in with a suit on and they're like, "Derrick, here's your schedule for the day. Here's what we're doing today with the kids." "Alright. Let's get this taken care of." I want to be able to be hands-on in there, be involved, see what's happening and how, be a part of it.

I want to make change. I want to have the facilities to start with—my family able to work there if they want to, everybody's kids able to go up there. Not exactly a Boys & Girls Club, but something where you have a facility. If you wanna do something for the kids in the neighborhood, you just block off hours for them. So from 9:00–12:00, you have a league going on. Or you have workouts going on. It's blocked off. From 12:00–1:00, the kids in the area get the gym. So they know at a certain time that this is their court, and you do that like two times a day, where they get to do whatever they want in the gym and experience it that way.

One reason I like to be in L.A. in the summer is to talk to Magic, for him to give me the connection to people who own the buildings, the real estate, for how he goes about what he does. Look at Magic's involvement with the kids, like the movie theaters. I love movie theaters, and I've been to plenty of his.

I feel I always take care of people, because that was the way growing up. You had to look out for others to survive— in our house, in our neighborhood. I always say, "Do it the right way, where I don't use my money, my savings. I always use the money that I get coming in. Don't touch what's there." I will say, it keeps me humble to see the numbers on those statements. But I do live a simple life.

I'm a simple eater. I don't eat fish or steak. I only eat turkey and chicken. My mom cooked growing up, she liked to cook. I ate a lot more then, but that's one of the reasons I think I don't eat steak anymore. Because when you're younger, you're buying steak, but what's the grade of the steak, the quality? We were buying this steak—or whatever it really was—from the corner store. So you can only imagine how tough it was. I think that's what threw me off steak, that texture. It wasn't what you would call a quality steak. On game day, I always ate pasta, ate a sandwich. I was big on Subway sandwiches back in the day, then pasta and chicken or potatoes before a game and I'd be fine. I wouldn't eat the entire meal. Just half of it. Sometimes go out to eat after a game, but most of the time going back home and me and my friends talking, going over the game.

With Alaina, we go out anywhere to eat on the road. I like Italian food and Chinese food. We go out mostly when we're in New York, Miami, L.A., Boston, New Orleans, the majority of the big cities, Toronto. I'll go to movies by myself a lot on the road. Alaina, she doesn't like scary movies. So I'll go to a scary movie by myself. I love those kinds of movies. But as far as going to a restaurant, I have to have someone with me. I only like food like that, or I'll stay in the room if no one is with me. See a movie on the road, go back to the hotel. I never really have to disguise myself. I'm average height, not like 6'6", 6'8". I'm able to blend in if I put a hat on. I just look down and walk.

On the road in the league, I love the big environments. Like LeBron playing with the Lakers. Couldn't wait to play them. It reminds me of the outdoor games back in Chicago, everyone hanging all over the court, the yelling, the taunting. I love the oohs, the ahhs. I love when you make a basketball play and the crowd reaction tells you they understand, that they recognize what's going on in the game. It could look simple, but, "Oh shit, that was a good pass!" I love playing in places like that.

Like playing in Philly. They'd yell a lot of stuff. There was a guy who had his "Didn't take the SAT" sign up. You know the guy who would be writing on the board during the games?

He was scribbling. He was dying laughing when he showed it to me. I could respect it. I started laughing. I like that kind of stuff. That's why I always killed them when we played them in Philly. Boston, too. Good shooting arena. Lakers, Staples Center is great. I like Phoenix, Golden State, too.

People would yell stuff sometimes like in Philly and Boston, just, "You're garbage," that type of stuff. But I feed off it. "Alright, that's where we're at right now? Just watch this now. I'm going to score this next bucket and we'll see if you look at me the same way." You gotta feel it. It's good for the fans, too, to experience that. That's not me off the floor, but when I'm on the floor I turn into a different person. What do they say in Chicago? Not backing down. On the floor, I don't have to talk crazy. I don't have to say anything. I can show you.

I FELT I WAS BUILDING BACK UP, getting right toward the end in Chicago. But you could tell the karma—things were changing. You know when you are with someone and you're with them all the time, but things are, well, changing, and then someone else comes along? I felt like it was becoming that way with the Bulls with me, with Jimmy coming along. And Jimmy really wanted some things.

I always was cool with Jimmy, no matter what they were saying in the media. I was always cool with all my teammates. That's what it is having teammates. I never had a problem with Jimmy. No confrontation, no argument or anything. In fact, when Jimmy had his trade stuff come up in Minnesota, he was confiding in me and I was counseling him, understanding what he was going through, how it wasn't right. We were texting back and forth all the time. I was telling him not to let them take his leverage from him. I was talking to all my teammates then, more than I ever talked with any team. I understood that I was that vet, that I had to be the leader and talk, even though that's never been who I am.

People always wanted to make it something between me and Jimmy in Chicago, wanting to see us go at it and then step back and say, "Those guys are bad." Sort of light the match and then, "Let's watch two black guys fight it out."

Nah, nothing like that with me and Jimmy. But I will say it was a different Jimmy by the time I got to Minnesota. Not to say he was an asshole with the Bulls, but he was a more confident veteran in Minnesota. The trade stuff and camp, that was different. Remember, I did buy him that watch that time with the Bulls. Just to show, "Bro, I ain't whatever they may be saying." It was light love for a teammate. I think it cost like $15,000. When you're the veteran, sometimes you have to spoil your teammates. I've done other things like that. With my family, friends, teammates. Like I said, we like to be generous.

I knew things were changing with the Bulls, but I had to just play. I had another surgery at the end of the 2014 season, but I came back for the playoffs. Beat Milwaukee, though I cost us that one game on defense when Jerryd Bayless got by me for the score after my turnover. We won that series and then it was Bron again, and I thought we had them after my shot in Game 3. Don't think I called bank. Then Bron makes one in Game 4 and we can't finish it. But it shouldn't have mattered. We had that game won, but the refs weren't watching, or maybe watching and who knows, but they really hurt us. Another loss to Bron. But it does make you wonder.

That Game 3 shot was cool. I did have some reaction after making that shot. Just letting them know we're still here. You understand, we battled them for numerous years. Even if we had a better regular season, they'd stop us every time in the playoffs. Back and forth. Even when Bron went to Miami, same thing. It was just one of those things where it was like, "Man, we're still here fighting. This ain't gonna be a cakewalk." When you're playing against a guy like that, a team like that, you've got to keep fighting to show that resilience. And then in Game 4, come on, their coach, David Blatt, called timeout when they didn't have one. Should have been a technical and the game is over. We're up three games to one.

Hell yeah, I saw it. We knew right away. Thibs always tells you how many timeouts you have, how many they have, if they're gonna foul, the situation. You know with Thibs he always was the most prepared. Dude is all the way out on the court calling a timeout. Right in front of the ref. Everyone knows.

And then for Bron to hit the shot, it was like a double whammy. Like, "Oh! He hit the fucking shot!" You wanna have an outburst like a kid, like a Little League game you lose. Like the refs cheated you—you wanna cry out. But the way we always looked at it was there were more games and it's the league. But it shouldn't have come to that, because Blatt was right on the court crying for a timeout. We all saw that.

WE WERE ALL AWARE things weren't going good between Thibs and Bulls management. It was just that we felt we had a bond that was so close, we thought winning was gonna take care of it. Just win. Like anything else in this league, you win and everything gets swept under the rug. Thibs never said anything to us about that stuff. He's never gonna let you in on what he's personally going through.

But then they changed coaches after that season, and all of a sudden it just seemed like it was coming to an end for me in Chicago, too. Not that I wanted it or anyone said anything, but things were happening. Like, the first practice and I get that elbow in the face from Taj and I'm seeing double for months. Seem like a sign to you?

I come back and I had to shoot with one eye. No bullshit, one eye. I came back early so I wouldn't lose my wind, the conditioning I had built up by then. I tried to fight through it and I think I played well that season despite going through that. But it's tough trying to go out there and piece your vision together, trying to figure out the depth of the rim. I started shooting bank shots. I had to try something.

But the critics were growing. I felt I'd made a lot of progress. I think I played 40 out of 43 games until the knee thing after the All-Star Game, and then came back for the last four or five before the playoffs. Then in Fred Hoiberg's first season, I ended up playing 66 games. So I'm playing consecutive games, showing I can be out there, but the vibe was different, a lot of things going on.

When Taj elbowed me in camp I also chipped nine teeth. I had headaches after that, like a migraine. I had to have eye therapy, where you go in and read these letters and look at these certain shapes to get your range back. I was doing that for months.

In some ways that one was the worst, because I wasn't allowed to get my blood pressure up. I couldn't have sex. Because if your blood pressure rose, it messed with your eye. They told me I can't be excited. Can't watch movies. They basically want you alone doing nothing, because if blood gets in there, it can be damaged and permanent. That went for maybe three weeks, a month.

Hey, it's just my story. I don't think people know me like that, but I feel like they can feel it, feel something about me they can relate to. You know, things look good outside sometimes, but inside you're struggling.

Jo got hurt that last season about halfway through and was out, Jimmy and Fred got into it, then Jimmy and Jo. We started losing and things were getting away. Jimmy wanted to be playing point guard. Different direction and all that. Actually, I was cool because I was playing those consecutive games. That was important to me. Lots of weird stuff was going on, though. I wasn't sure what it was about, but Jimmy didn't dress with us. That season he was always dressing with the coaches, didn't stay in the locker room. Got to say, I never did see that before. To separate yourself from the team. How the hell do you think we're a team when that's going on? Of course, I got the blame. But Jo saw it, he and Jimmy were at it. There was a lot of fracturing.

We were looking like we might miss the playoffs and we had a team meeting near the end of the season—never needed to have those before with the Bulls. It was Jimmy and Jo talking. I never say nothing in meetings because they always get leaked. Jo wasn't playing. So he really didn't know what the heck was going on. I sit there and act like I don't know what's going on, just take it all in, but I know exactly what happened.

Jo called me out for not speaking up, said I'm one of the leaders on the team and all. The reality of this was that it wasn't my fault. First off, "Jo, you're not here. So you shouldn't be saying anything. Period." But I let him speak because I didn't want an argument. I just wanted to hear everything said and then I was gonna have my conversation with BJ and we were gonna discuss a plan. Then Jimmy ended up snapping on the coaching staff. They didn't say anything though.

Just ended up with Jimmy and Jo arguing. Some crazy stuff that season.

Then it gets to the end of the season and even though I don't know I'm gone, it seems like I'm next. With all the stuff going on that season and the media and all, I was angry and you'd think I was ready. But I wasn't. I was emotional when I heard about the trade. I broke down. It was like a death in a way, leaving Chicago. I'd thought about it, but I don't think I really believed it would happen, even with everything that was going on. It was tough.

It was a great time with the Bulls overall. Including even playing basketball at the White House. Can you imagine something like that happening? Got my guy there with me, Joakim, so he made me even more comfortable. We were just sitting there chatting with President Obama, taking in the whole vibe. I've got the pictures, so that's something I'll be able to keep for my kids. Talking about the city, talking about the team. President Obama, he even knew little things about the team. I didn't know he was a big fan like that until I met him in person. But actually hearing the way he talked about the team, you could tell he knew about it.

Then he asked me to go to a fundraiser at Navy Pier. I'm thinking I'm coming there to see him talk his ass off. BJ pulls me to the side and says they might want you to do an introduction. I'm like, "I'm not ready, man. What you mean? Why didn't they tell me before I came?" Playing before 20,000 people, that's nothing compared to how nervous I was getting on that stage. This is like a once-in-a-lifetime moment. I went up there and I did it. BJ and my best friend Randall were behind me for support in case I couldn't say something.

Things kept getting weird right up to the end though. It's the last two games and we're out of the playoffs, but the Bulls say I have to play. I got through this season and I don't want to risk anything and, really, I'm still not quite right, so we told the Bulls we wanted to have a meeting.

Me and Reggie went in to talk with the Bulls about those last two games. We went up to the office and they let me vent. I had some things to say; it was cathartic.

It was two games. You see me put in all that work to get back, play with a broken face. Why would I lie about an injury for two games? What's wrong with that? So we went up to the office. I'm like, "I already went through a shitload of injuries. It's two games. And the two games aren't going to put us in the playoffs." You know how losing teams are. I felt healthy enough. Not great, but is it worth the risk for two games? They hit us with, "Do it for the fans." Do it for the fans? Fuck it. My brother stopped 'em right away. "What you mean, fans? These two games are not gonna mean anything."

Of course, those last two games, funny, what position did Jimmy play? Point guard. I had to laugh. No, it didn't bother me. I knew what it was. I'm not dumb.

That's the way it goes. Way it was for me then, way it was for Jimmy later in Minnesota. I saw the summer after I got there, he turned down the $110 million from the Wolves. At

29 years old? With knee problems? They're going to throw that back at you, make you look like all you care about is the money. I know. And they did that to Jimmy, tried to make him the bad guy. Any injury now they're throwing it at you. "We wanna see what we're paying for first."

I could see it happening. With the Bulls it was becoming, "We've gotta change the direction of the team."

I didn't totally get it at the time. A couple weeks after we had that little interaction, BJ said, "Alright, my man. I keep hearing New York." Then that shit went quiet. Then a call came in that I'm traded.

It was time. But it also was tough, like the bottom dropping out. I was doing my documentary at the time and it got me. I broke down crying, really. No lie. I know everything that was happening, but it was Chicago. It was me, what made me. Right when I was having that filming done. It was tough, like when I was in the hospital with my mom after the ACL injury. Felt like it was the end all over again, another twist, even though I knew I still was going to be playing.

At the end of that meeting about the last two games, we really all were cool. "This is all just miscommunication. All you had to do was just tell us that." Laughing at the end and everything. I wasn't yelling at them or nothing. I was just talking to them, like a man. I was a young man at that time standing up for myself. I was proud of what I did. "Y'all think I'm quiet. I know you probably all think I'm dumb, but I know what's going on."

Maybe they got scared of that. Even with this book, I know people are going to be surprised just to hear me talk. If I say the ABCs they'll be like "Ooh!" I should just have a video of me saying the ABCs and people will start clapping. But that doesn't bother me. That's why it's funny. Because you really don't know me, so you're gonna be blown away by anything I say.

I told them everything I saw. I don't usually say much, but I see. I was a young man. My big bro got to see me in the business atmosphere and handle it professionally. I felt good about the way I handled it, said what I had to, stood up for myself. And then we were cool.

I know what some people think. Happens with a lot of basketball players. When I talk to people, they're amazed I can even talk. It also amazes me sometimes. Like, "Wow, you really thought I was dumb." But that's also what makes my job the best job in the world. I didn't have to pretend, didn't have to go in and kick somebody's ass or pretend I like or didn't like somebody. I was blessed enough to be me and be comfortable being the way I am. I've been fortunate enough to succeed being that way. It's a blessing.

I gotta respect the Bulls for sending me to New York when they could have sent me anywhere else. Great market, big city, great fans, short flight to Chicago. Sure, I wanted to stay in Chicago, but I was happy, really, that the Bulls still looked out for me that way. I respected them for that. They could have sent me, like Cleveland did, to Utah. That's one of the reasons I like to go back and just shoot the shit with them guys there. Gotta respect that part of it. Sending me to another big market, a place where I thought we could win. Just never got that championship for my hometown. It's all love.

And I always say, Jerry Reinsdorf really taught me a lot, showed me something different, showed me how to handle yourself with money, showed me about treating people the right way. Still drives himself to work in a Cadillac. I like that.

LOOK, THIS WAS THE BUSINESS I CHOSE. So, I really can't complain too much about it. I never put up a tweet or something to say I hate the media. Nothing like that. Somebody asks me something, I give them an honest answer. That's always the way I was. But suddenly it's like, "Oh my god, I can't believe he's saying that!" I've had a wild time with the media and I never thought that would happen.

I don't know if anyone ever had media stuff like I did. I'm not saying guys don't go through all sorts of tough things with the media, but in your hometown like that? Tell me who that's happened to. And what did I do? I didn't beat anybody or steal something or hurt someone. I said some stuff maybe the way you didn't like to hear it or didn't think it sounded right, but it was just me telling you straight.

I never was good at playing the game—you know, the media game. I'm not a bullshitter. If I don't like you, I'm not gonna talk to you or you're just gonna feel it. I'm not gonna

bullshit you and laugh in your face with you. With me growing up and seeing everything, I tried to avoid becoming a
bullshitter.

The problem was I was already in a profession where
everybody is. So should I be like that or be like me? I'm trying to tell you how I feel, and maybe it doesn't come out the
way you want to hear it. But people understand. I'm the bad
guy? It's not like I'm the only one; plenty of people go through
it. I know that. I saw what happened with Bron and Miami.
KD got a lot of stuff going to the Warriors. It's just funny
the way it happened in Chicago. One minute I'm their favorite, the kid who made it, then I'm a bad guy? Leave? Why?

Obviously, my injuries had a lot to do with it. But, hey,
I'm the one injured; it's my career. I was the one in the hospital thinking maybe that was the end. So you think about
things. I'm what, 24? They're thinking I don't want to play.
I'm trying to get back to play, but I really can't. Now you see
how long it takes, but nobody wanted to hear it back then.

Then there were those times I said some things I was
thinking and maybe they didn't come out like they wanted
to hear, but I was just being straight, no bullshit. What, you
can't take it? I'm saying what everyone else says.

One time was when I came back after missing that whole
season after going down in Portland. So I say—and I looked
it up to see how it came out—"I feel I've been managing
myself pretty good. I know a lot of people get mad when they
see me sit out. But I think a lot of people don't understand

that when I sit out, it's not because of this year. I'm thinking about long-term. I'm thinking about after I'm done with basketball, having graduations to go to, having meetings to go to. I don't want to be in my meetings all sore or be at my son's graduation all sore just because of something I did in the past. Just learning and being smart."

Then the next year after it was all summer, everyone's talking about what's going to happen with the salary cap, and you saw some guys get these crazy deals. And so I'm just trying to say to the media, sort of like, "Hey, I'm letting you guys know." You know, no bullshit. It was, "This whole summer I had tunnel vision." My mindset was just making sure that I was working out every day, spending as much time as possible with my son, focusing on those two things. Making sure my family is financially stable, as far as seeing all the money that they're passing out in this league.

I was just telling the truth, just knowing that my day will be coming up soon. That money is for my children and their future, so that's what I'm thinking about. When you talk about that much money, the only thing you can do is prepare for it. I'm trying to prepare not only myself but my family. Just putting out there what all of us were thinking. Even though we're alright, we're comfortable, when you talk about that amount of dollars, I think it raises everyone's eyebrows, so there's nothing wrong with being overprepared.

My critics always get mad when I show love for myself or show that I care about myself. That's all it was. In this position, are you supposed to be a slave to the game? And to the system? Your body and health is the last thing you should care about? When in reality that should be number one. That's all I was saying, same thing everyone else says.

I'm saying that now, but when I was younger I said how I felt at the time. But what was I showing you? I kept coming back to play, to stand up. I didn't run from the media, have people block me off so you couldn't see me, talk to me. I was there. So what's so wrong with what I said, caring about your health, your family, wanting to make sure you can have your health in your life for your family, my son? And I swear to God, I just recently heard Shaq talking about feeling the same thing during his career, same stuff I said, talking about his kids, all that. And they were killing me on their TNT show back in the day over this. And Barkley, you know all the stuff he did—getting arrested—like he knows about doing the right thing? They asked Shaq about his son going to college and he was like, "Oh, I want to be able to go to his college games." Isn't that the same thing?

You saw the same thing with Kawhi in his last season with the Spurs. Where it's like, "What's going on?" What's different about his situation is that they can still make money off him. So he was safer. They felt with me, "He's done." You know what I mean? "We don't need him anymore, rate him down." There were some people in the media who went off about Kawhi, but the league, they know they can still make money off him so they're not going to bash his name. With me, it was like, "He's already had the injury. We're moving on."

People think I'm a cocky, reckless, unruly person. That's not me. It's for my son and that's all I was trying to say. He's the big reason I'm playing this game. My dad wasn't around. My mom was that figure for me. I want to be the example to my son, the dad I didn't have. He's going to do what he wants to do, but someday he's going to be like, "Damn, Pops was right." It's going to hit him one day.

YOU KNOW, THE THING IS I NEVER WANTED TO BE FAMOUS. But like BJ once told me, I'm a contradiction. That I have this quiet personality but the flashy game. I play flashy, the oohs and aahs, but then I don't want the attention. When you play like that people think that's who you are and they want you to be that. But that's not me. I never wanted to tap into the fame. But it's who they want you to be, and then you try to be yourself and that's not the right thing for them. "No, you be that guy!" Then you say some stuff and it's, "No, we don't like him that way."

Look, that start of the season when I talked openly about free agency, I was thinking about the money, like everybody was. It was the TV money. All the players were talking about it that summer in L.A. Our agents were telling us. So many players are in L.A. and that's what you're hearing. So then people ask me what's going on and I tell them. But that's when they're also counting my pockets. Hey, you're a grown man worried about another grown man's money? Come on. I'm getting the insight from BJ about, "Hey, that TV money is coming soon and it's going to change everything." So we shouldn't talk about that?

I can't help the fact I'm getting the inside scoop on shit and that I understand what it will mean. Me just being honest with y'all. I'm explaining, it's not that I don't care about my teammates. Come on, I've always been the guy trying to help my teammates get a better chance for a scholarship, for the league. Yeah, I'm training hard because I see what's ahead. I had a great summer in 2015. I've got a chance to really get this money right here.

Yes, I'm gonna talk about it. Why not? Who isn't also playing for the money? And I always said I wanted to stay with the Bulls, not be some free agent running around to teams, which is any player's right. My goal is to achieve so that the kids watching me are like, "Damn, y'all got something going on over here." I'm not into money like that. I love it because I can take care of my family, I can do things for people, for the kids. So how come with me they say I've got enough? Not the business guy or the computer guy or the Apple guy? That's why I say, "Why are you watching my pockets?" You want me to play dumb to the fact that $24 billion is coming into the league next year?

I know you're not supposed to talk about money, and money isn't what drives us into this game, but players talk about money. I've been around working people. Who at your job isn't talking about money, what this one makes, what that one makes? How about the big corporate CEOs and the money they make? How much you hear people saying they shouldn't make that money? So why shouldn't basketball players make money? I know the amounts are crazy, but we're working for someone, too. The people should feel closer to us than they do the owners.

I watch a lot of documentaries and you see about the stuff with the railroads and the oil companies back in the old days and how the owners took advantage of the workers, and then they'd give some workers more to try to turn the workers on the bottom against them so the owners were safe on top. Same thing. Like what Oscar Robertson and those guys did for the players back in the '70s, fighting for the right to be free agents. If you didn't stand up and say something and talk about it, then the owners get to keep everything. I know NBA players are not like regular union guys, but we work for people and we talk about money. It doesn't mean we don't care or don't work hard or play hard. We do.

Like when I got that first big contact from the Bulls after winning the MVP and after the lockout, I didn't understand how big it was at the time. But I'll tell you one thing I've always been proud of is having a rule in the league from that, the Derrick Rose Rule, in the CBA. I have to thank my agents, Arn Tellem and BJ, for that. They always treated me like family. You know how close I am with BJ, and Arn is still like family for me. It was the rule they put in where a guy could get 30 percent of the salary cap. I was the only one eligible at the time because of the MVP award. Others became eligible, but it's more than just the money. It shows that if you grind you will get a percentage of what the cap is, a percentage of the profits of the business, which is the right thing.

This is what guys like Oscar were fighting for. Everyone was saying they were crazy or greedy, but they were fighting to control their own careers, fighting for us, for the future. How lucky we were that players so long ago understood what this all would mean. The Rose Rule? It probably still won't hit me until I'm gone, but to know I actually have a rule under my name is amazing, an honor.

Just getting my rookie contract was amazing. To get that kind of money, I couldn't fathom that, and when I got the Adidas deal I actually started to get nervous. Me and my friends were talking in a room and they were saying how after I got this money everything was gonna change. Saying I wasn't gonna be able to walk down the street, do this anymore, do that anymore. We were laughing about it, but it scared me.

But you know how it works. At that time my name was headlines, injuries, was the MVP. "Is he done?" Anything with my name at that time was hot, anything I said. Especially if I talked honest. They love when I talked honest. It's like, "Alright, now we got ya." But what could I do? Players like MJ could go to Ahmad Rashad for a special interview and all his stuff was straightened out. Kobe could go to Stephen A. LeBron can go to who, the guy from *Sports Illustrated*, to say what he meant. Who was my reporter?

I'm in a market where if I say something—no matter what it was—it seemed like they were gonna twist my story. I don't know why. It's my hometown. I'm telling you the honest truth. I hear players now say, "I want to be able to walk when I'm older." When I said it, it was like, "You're thinking about yourself and not your team. Hey, you're not fully invested." And I'm working like that and going through rehab and rehab and rehab. What was the point of me harping on it when they kept coming up with shit? So, I said the truth sometimes.

I got quiet, quieter, and just talked to my friends a lot. I'll admit it. "They're trying to trick you," they'd tell me. Certain times, when you heard me stand on certain issues or say things, it's like, "I'm not letting nobody control me. I'll say what I want to say. I'm not harming nobody but being honest. Y'all say y'all want this honesty. But in reality, you don't. You want to hear what you want to hear." I'm playing on this uneven, unbalanced field. Like, you don't know who to trust, you just want to play ball. I know it's just some people in the media, but you hate it for your family when your name is out there like that.

Players understand. I appreciated what Jabari Parker said when he had his press conference in July 2018, when he came to the Bulls. Said I was one of the best from Chicago, appreciated what I accomplished. It's big to hear that compliment. My relationship with the media is different than with a lot of other players. I watch what I say. But to hear him say that and hear other people comment about it, it made me feel good.

I was in a different state of mind back then, after the injuries, and I felt like I couldn't back down. You know, how I was raised in Chicago, I felt like I was being attacked, so I wasn't backing down to enemies. I decided I wasn't giving no elaborate answers. I changed. I decided, "I'm gonna act like I don't want to be there. Because you're fucking harassing me every day on purpose." I was mad.

I never really thought about how I was supposed to be the Chicago favorite until I got to New York. Looking back on it, I felt fortunate to be in a new environment, being there with new people. I was cool with it. The media in New York asked questions—and yeah, some were crazy questions—but outside of that it wasn't an everyday thing like back in Chicago, where they were trying to investigate you or trying to figure out some shit that wasn't there.

Was it the money? "You're making $20 million. Why ain't you playing?" Nobody felt like they had control over me, and I think that bothered them. So, I decided I'm not giving special interviews, or giving them little hints about what's going on with the team.

You see, these are just men and women in the media who write about you every day. They're human, too. And some of them are maybe jealous and they just show that jealousy through what they type on a computer. At your interviews, asking you bullshit where you know it's gonna start something. Some were just blatant with it. I'd never had that anywhere. Where someone asks you a question like that and everybody's like, "Damn, I can't believe he asked you that." But then no one says anything. They wait to see, "Oh, what's he gonna say?" Clickbait, I guess.

I knew what was going on. But I'm not big on Instagram or Twitter or any of that. I'll look at my friends' sometimes to see what's going on, but that's it. The people on there talking shit, like, who cares? But it did get to a point where I felt like I had to defend myself.

If I was mad at anything, I was mad nobody had my back. I felt like I was fighting it myself. I felt like, I'm a part of your franchise, I'm a part of your association, one of your players that you're making money off is getting harassed by the media, and you can't say anything? Put a memo out saying, "You guys can't do this to him. Just stop." They can't do that? That's how I felt. Maybe it's not possible for them to do that, but I felt I was by myself. I felt like if it was a situation where somebody was talking about someone in the league, then the league would say something. But if I mentioned it, they'd make it a big problem.

It was getting crazy. I get my face smashed to start that last season in Chicago, a bubble under the eye, but they criticized me for that, too. Come on, man. You got one eye and they still talk shit about you? Makes me laugh when I think back about it. Really?

It made me think, even if I would have accomplished something great there, would it be the same anymore? What would it be like? That's why I realized I was the one who had to get a grip. "Alright, don't drive yourself crazy, because these people really don't know what's going on. They don't know what you're really going through."

After a while, I stopped listening. My family members knew, don't bring anything up to me that's gonna drain me, stress me out. I don't wanna hear about no articles. If I stumble across that article, let me handle that.

We all know media is a part of this life, and with the media comes the attention and everything, and the league makes money and we make money. I get it. But you always hope it's at least fair.

It got to, for me, "Why should I open up and tell them? Why should I give you something when you're just gonna shit on the story, anyway, and tell it the way you want?" But at the same time I didn't like what it was doing to me, the person I was becoming. It wasn't me. But that shit can change you. I learned that. Don't let it. You're still the one to be the model for your family, for the kids, for your son. You be the better person, the one who treats others right even if you feel you don't get treated that way. I get it. It's cool.

I think of those people asking me for autographs and talking shit behind my back. I think of Shaq and Charles and them on TNT telling me to go away and then when I play better acting like they were always behind me. And I think of the way I was being at that time, keeping it all in, hiding my real self. For me, I never want to be that type of person. That's the message I want to send to others, period. Be who you're gonna be. It's a lesson. Don't go in that direction. They can see that I'm not perfect, but they also can see somebody that's trying. That's who I want to be.

I regretted the way I acted. I was wrong. I got caught up. With me having that attitude in Chicago, the way that I handled that whole situation, I should have been the bigger person. But I was too young at the time. I learned to take that higher road. Don't let them bring you down. Sure, I can give my son money, but it's also these lessons that are important. I had to learn. Chicago will always be in me, who I am. It's home.

It was tough. It did hurt, I'll admit that. But you have to go through the pain sometimes to get where you want. It changed me, to where I wasn't so aggressive anymore. Not that it's my music, but I took a quote I once read from Frank Sinatra. He said the best revenge is success. That's what I decided I would do. I took that anger and decided to prove people wrong, but not say anything. You can cheer, you can down-talk. For me, I'll just show you.

12

I REALLY THOUGHT WE WERE GOING TO HAVE A SPECIAL TEAM in New York. We've got Carmelo Anthony and Kristaps Porzingis, signed Joakim, some good guys off the bench, had Phil Jackson running the show, and Jeff Hornacek's a good coach. Plus, Jo's from New York, it's his hometown, and we played numerous years together in Chicago, so now I don't have to worry about trying to blend in or really go out there and try to force myself on someone when I've already got a friend.

Phil was always good. We didn't talk that much, but the times we did talk he talked like he felt I knew the game. So that always felt great. Whenever I did talk to him, it would be little things like him talking about feeding it to the post. He'd ask what type of pass you got to throw. I'd finish his sentence, like, "Not a bounce pass, a lob pass. You don't want a big bending over and all that." So he knew that I saw the game and he talked to me like I was a coach.

We had that game early in the season in Chicago, me and Jo going back, and we won a tough game against a good team. But every game really was big for me. Every game felt like that because I felt it was going to be a big year, for leaving Chicago, for going to New York, the Garden, where everyone loves to play, great fans, big media. I had such high expectations for the team before I got there. I really wanted to perform every game. New York is the biggest market. Why not try to spark something there and have the chance?

I thought things were lined up for us to have a hell of a year. It turned out to be the total opposite. So that was kind of devastating. But I did love the way I performed that year. Played 64 games after playing 66 the previous year in Chicago. And didn't play those last two in Chicago. So, I was playing consecutive games again, which is what I wanted to do. Lots of people didn't see it that way, thought I still was injured. But I was playing regular. To go somewhere else and play 60-something games in back-to-back seasons, I felt I finally had put that behind me.

But it was a late start to that season with the trial, the assault case when we were found not liable by a jury in Los Angeles.

I don't know what I'm supposed to say, because there still are appeals. A California Court of Appeals, I know, heard oral arguments in November 2018. It was reported that the judge said to the plaintiff's attorney, "The defendants, as I look at the record, had powerful defenses to that presentation, which at the end of the day, the jury bought. You had a nine-day trial and this jury was out what, 15 minutes? And you lose on every single claim. The jury just didn't buy your case. No trial is perfect, but your evidence concerning the night in question came in and the jury had an opportunity to hear that."

Remember, I did go to trial. I know it was a civil trial, but I went before a jury. I stood up to it. I guess you could say going through it was good, from the standpoint that it helped me focus my energy on what's important, my priorities. That's life changing. Just the way I go about things.

I don't want anything to ever be like that again, where they're saying that about me. I don't want my name near that kind of stuff at all. I'm quiet, but it did open my eyes to what's going on in the world and what can happen to you.

This was a woman who wasn't telling the truth. Look, I was raised by my mom and my grandma. Any woman who I have ever encountered, ever, who I've ever been with, ask them, I would never be the aggressor. Because of my mom and my grandmother, it's my respect for women. I feel like with them raising me and their character, what that imparted to me, I'd never be over a woman, like groping a woman, where I have to use her. I never approached women that way.

So, I didn't see it coming, that this could happen. I learned from that. But it's also what my mom had to endure. She just knew it wasn't the truth. It was something where she didn't harp on it. Told me to focus on what I need to focus on.

I also had my son to think about. Probably, if I had no kids, I wouldn't have cared. But me having him, I don't want him to ever stumble on what was said. And then if you settle or don't say anything, it's like you're admitting you did something wrong, raped a woman. I didn't.

People were telling me to settle, and some sponsors walked away. That's okay. People just step away, which they have every right to do. I don't blame them, even if she had no evidence—zero. She was lying about this whole story. Makes it bad for other women, because this is no joke.

But this wasn't me. Not who I am or ever was. And you shouldn't have to pay off someone just so they won't lie about you. Is that right? That's why I went to court. There were a lot of bad articles that were going to be written, but I didn't have anything to hide. If things were fair, I knew I would be alright. I also knew I had my whole contract on the line. But I was just thinking about my pride, my integrity. I was raised by my mom, my grandmother, my brother. This was about them, too.

At first, I'll admit I didn't take it serious enough. I didn't know anything about court. I'm thinking we're gonna go there and they're gonna easily see. We're gonna go there for a day and that's gonna be it. I don't watch *48 Hours, CSI, Law & Order*, none of those shows. I didn't watch the O.J. case. I was too young to keep up with it. I was a novice to all of it. I don't know anything about defamation and all this stuff they're talking about. I'm just fighting like I didn't do it.

When they started telling me about it, I'm like, "Alright, this is gonna be over quick." I'm not thinking it's gonna be out to the public like that. So when it happened, I just had to deal with it. I was thinking it was gonna be two days; ended up being two weeks.

But it did open my eyes. I just wanted to know what I had to do in court. No, I'm going to fight it for me, for my family, for my son.

They told me I could settle for this amount, but I told them, "No, I didn't do anything." First off, I'm not thinking about paying you, because I didn't do what you said. And second, I felt like, "If I settle, she'll always want more." That's what I'm thinking about, too. I ended up telling BJ that I wanted to fight it.

He told me, "It's gonna be a lot of press that comes with it." They tried to talk me out of it.

It's integrity, really. Part of being raised by my mom and my grandmother. Growing up with my grandmother, we learned how to treat women. My mom was so hurt. She knew it was fake right away. Come on, man. I'm the enabler. I'm the one who'll let you get away with a certain amount. But there's a boiling point with everyone. There were all the charges, the accusations. But I felt like it was worth it to try to clear my name.

It was hard prepping for it. You're in the room with your lawyers and they're going over questions as if they're her lawyers, not yours. Not to be rude, but our lawyers were beating them every day in court. But the media, the way they were putting it out sometimes, they made it seem like she had a chance. If you were in that courtroom every day, you wouldn't think so.

I told the jury when I had the opportunity. I had nothing to hide. You talk about a kid who never sold drugs, nothing. I put myself in that position. So I've got to fight it. The people on the jury, they saw this was a money grab. I'm happy they saw it that way, because that was something I was trying to get across right from the beginning.

It just all made for this crazy season. I had to miss some of the preseason with the trial and that's what I was concentrating on most. I had to focus on myself, my image, my character. That's a city where you can get tempted, New York, but I wasn't getting involved in any of that. It's some serious stuff I was involved in; you don't take that stuff casual.

WITH THE BASKETBALL, the way Phil had talked, and with Jo and Melo, I really thought we were going to do something.

But when it came to the basketball, I knew right away that we were shit.

I played through it, 60-some games, but I could tell right away it wasn't the season I was expecting. Lot of different priorities. Melo's there. You know how he plays. Can't change that. That's what I realized being there. And he's a great dude;

I loved being around Melo. He ain't gonna rub you the wrong way. Great dude, great spirit, great person, great teammate.

I don't say much, but Phil could tell. Phil was telling me to be patient. He said I had a lot going on with the trial and all. He was honest with me. Everything he talked to me about, he was honest, I'll say that. Our relationship was a little weird, though. He was cool the whole time I was there, but he wanted that $60 million he was owed by the Knicks.

As for me, I liked Phil, but, come on, man, you're still running the triangle? He was still forcing them to run it. I'm a slasher, a driving point guard. The triangle is okay, but not for the personnel we had. Melo couldn't play that way, didn't want to.

With me leaving Chicago, I really was into the game, really wanted to do something. New York with Jo and Phil and Melo and leaving Chicago, it just sounded like it was going to be special. Getting back to winning.

I had high expectations and I wanted to perform. I felt the spark. But we never had a flow on the offensive or defensive end. I felt like being there we never did the extra things to win the game, make the hustle play or the extra pass. We played numerous games where we'd hit a point where it just all fell apart. We had an alright start, playing around .500 ball into December, but you could tell it was getting worse. We knew it was only a matter of time.

Coming in, especially in the East, a team like that you know can compete, a team with that talent. They were trying to do it for Melo; he didn't want to start over so they wanted to get the veterans for him. But he can't play with a lot of guys, he's gotta be the main guy. Supposed to be a top-five team. You should just fall into winning games with that much talent, but we were struggling to stay in it at halftime. It was frustrating, but at the same time all of it was out of our control. Jo and I used to talk about that all the time. Phil wanted us to play a certain way and we had to listen. What can you do?

Early on in the season, Phil really didn't force anything. But as time went on, it converted all the way to the triangle and we played through that almost the whole year. For the team we had, I think deep down Hornacek really wanted to play that more up-tempo style. But being in that position, being a new head coach, having to listen to the front office, it's hard on that coach to say something. He's moved around, he'd been fired in Phoenix. I guess Hornacek got tired of hearing about it, having meetings about it, so he just said, "We're gonna do it and see."

It also took a lot out of us. It's hard to go into games knowing there's a point during the game where the game slips away. You can feel it. The whole team can feel it. But that was every other night.

There were times during a game where we would play free. And it didn't matter what we did. We'd end up coming back, and Phil would be like, "What's that?" I remember one time we beat Boston and he told Hornacek he didn't like the way we finished that game. We ended up winning the game. Melo got kicked out the game or something like that, something crazy, but Phil didn't like the way we finished that game. It's like, "Damn, in the league you're happy to get a win."

Most coaches come in and they're like, "That was ugly, but bring it in! Enjoy your night. Nothing crazy tonight." You know what I mean? Enjoy it because it's hard to even get one win in this league. I've talked to Kobe about the triangle—you saw it with the Bulls and MJ, you can do it and it works—but we were a new team with new players and a new coach, and because of Melo and the way he played, we needed to do something now, and you need some time with that offense.

I ACTUALLY LOVED MY EXPERIENCE being in New York. Cool place. With the way things were the last couple of years in Chicago, I saw I needed a break.

When I left the Knicks that day in January 2017, that's what it was about. I just needed to go home.

I went to the crib with my mom. Everybody came over to the house to talk. That's the first time, one of the few times, where we sat down as a whole family and had a serious discussion like that.

I had decided I was done playing. I saw the same thing that was happening with the Bulls was going on with New York. I could tell that the season wasn't going to be the season everyone thought, that I thought. I didn't know if I wanted to hoop anymore. Especially when it started to feel like a business. Of course, you know it's a business. They always say that. But you know it's also hoopin'. But it had started to feel like all business, no joy. That's when I wanted out. I wasn't having fun.

The court case probably had something to do with it when I think back on it, but the love wasn't the same. I had too many distractions.

Yes, a lot of that falls on myself. I didn't have to leave, but at the time it felt like I was the only one going through what I was going through. My family talked me into going back.

It was the family, a long conversation, a lot of crying, yelling. It was crazy, but it's good to know they were behind me. It was a mixed feeling in the room; they know me and they know I know what I want to do. You got one group saying that and you got one group who's like, "Fuck that! You gotta get through. You gotta play the games."

That's when I realized it was a game within the game. I wasn't good at playing the game, at bullshitting. Like I said, with me growing up where and how I did and seeing everything, I tried to avoid becoming someone who did that. But the profession I was now in kind of demands it.

I felt like nobody could understand me, but my mom and brothers helped me. Everybody has jobs they don't want. But they still have to take care of their responsibilities, and that's where they let me know I was looking at it in a selfish way. I had to find the love of basketball again, and I would. It would be through PJ, my kids.

I've got enough money saved for lifetimes. I'm like, "Fuck this. Mistreat me, okay. I don't care. I'm out." That was a selfish way of looking at it. Because the things I would have stepped away from could have easily helped us financially, could've made us more comfortable in the future and enabled me to do things for others besides the family.

The question coming to me now was, "Did I want to keep moving because I was going to be a free agent? Would they keep me?" From sitting down and talking to the family, it was going over the pros and cons of everything. We came up with a list and figured it out. It was about me just sucking it up, listening to my family, and understanding where they were coming from.

It's still hard for me to overlook the business side of basketball. I naturally love the game. There's something about the game—just playing it—that draws me to it. I've always been obsessed with it. But then the business side, where you get put in a position where you feel like you're getting used, that's the part that's been hard for me to deal with.

My mom's always going to tell me to fight, say motherly things, try to encourage me to keep going. But I'm so stubborn and headstrong. They know at the end of the day I'm probably going to end up doing what I wanna do. That's why my family always laughed when everyone would say Reggie or someone was making me do what they wanted me to do.

They knew that was a joke, but I'm not gonna do it in a disrespectful way. I hear everybody out and adjust it the way I want it and make clear it's going to be a respectful decision.

It always comes from me being comfortable. Questioning if I wanted to hoop. Like, I'm saying there's more to me than just basketball. I'm more than just a hooper. That's actually also what made me want to write a book, do my documentary—solely by myself. It's about me going out to show people I'm more than just a hooper.

I don't want to be seen as me dancing in your face in a little commercial or whatever. I want you to see business deals when you read about me in the paper—that I did business deals, that I have my money, that I can help kids, help people in the community.

I was so frustrated then and I was quick to pull the trigger on it, a little too quick, I realized. My family was like, "You don't even have a plan. You don't have nothing set up right now. Even though you're financially stable, how are you going to transition?"

My family and friends—a small group—are for me like the president's cabinet. That's where the trust is, in these people, and I'm just one of them—not more special or important.

That's also why it was more complicated with one of my oldest and closest friends dropping out around that time. I don't want to say who it was, but it was someone who I grew up with, went back with to just about the beginning, so it was tough.

I pride myself on my loyalty, but then for someone to come out of left field like that, saying he wanted to show his own independence, it made me feel like I was the problem. That really hurt, with someone you are so close with. It's like losing a family member.

I always looked at it like we were all in this together. I never looked at it like it was just mine. I've always looked at my life and career as, we all made it together. I'm not that type of dude where I'm gonna be the only one looking fly or fresh or whatever and the people around me are looking bummy. Everybody is going to be comfortable around me and I'm not gonna go around crazy. I've always tried, and that was through my mom, to treat everyone how I would want to be treated.

People probably don't believe it, but that celebrity thing was a side I've always been blind to. That's why I am the way I am. I don't see that side. I know I'm regular, but a lot of people think being famous is something different.

Don't get me wrong, I'm cool with the perks. If you want to let me skip this line because I play basketball, good. If we talk, you'll see I'm much more than a hooper. The last thing you'll think when you talk to me is that I'm just a basketball player.

That's what grounds me, being able to realize you have to be more than what people see you as. And then manipulate it in a way where I don't lose myself in it, don't get caught up and think it's all about me.

So that's why what he said also kind of set me back, because I never thought it would come from someone so close—one of us. He was saying he needed to step away, that he had to figure out things on his own, which I felt like he could have done with the group, like I was trying to do, together. But he felt like he wanted to do it on his own.

I had to process that, which was tough, because I never had to think about that with one of my homeboys before. You question yourself. Then you retreat even more, because you wonder who will be next. You start expecting anything, which is the wrong way to deal with it. I realized that. I told him I wish him nothing but happiness and love and blessings. As a man, I've got to give you time to figure out what you need, and me to figure out where we're at.

At the end of the day, though, it was really about my son. I want to be able to hold him accountable. No reason you should have excuses about everything. So how can I ask him to be accountable if I'm making excuses, walking away because things aren't going well? I have responsibilities. And one of my responsibilities is to be a man and take care of my family. The money that I would have walked away from, my son and my family deserve that money. I can do good things with that money.

I worked my ass off to get that money. I earned it with my play. So why should I walk away from that when he could use that, when his kids could use that? The number one thing is I didn't want him to be growing up and feel like I let him down—or let the family down. I needed him to see that accountability.

I FEEL LIKE I PLAYED GREAT, but then had to have surgery again at the end of the season with the Knicks. By then I had changed my way of thinking. I really was in a great place. I wanted to be a Knick. It was just I had to have a surgery again. I had to prep myself for a rehab again. But I was now working with Judy Seto, this great lady who worked for the Lakers, the Dodgers, and I knew I would come out of this right.

I should have said something to someone that I was leaving to go home that day, but it was me just being me, me doing what I wanted to do. Looking back, I understood it probably worked against me with them. They felt they couldn't trust me, maybe. I wanted to go back to my family. Phil knew they—the Knicks—wouldn't have understood where I was coming from. Phil was always the coolest for me to deal with. But even my family didn't understand where I was coming from at that time. That's why I really needed to do what I wanted to do. And then come back because it was what I wanted to do after we all talked about it.

But the whole experience did open my eyes to a lot of things. New York, they could have given me my Bird rights before getting rid of me. That or working some kind of deal where, "Derrick, we're thinking of going in another direction. We're thinking of this Ntilikina kid in France. We respect you, but we wanna go in another direction." I would've respected that. Maybe something like what Sacramento did for George Hill, keep a veteran around to help the kids get going. Sacramento paid him and knew he was going to be the backup to De'Aaron Fox. You know what I mean? They looked out for him.

New York could have done the same thing. I would have done that. Me stepping away from the team that day had nothing to do with them; I was good with New York. But they didn't sign me, didn't even talk to me. No communication. I thought, "I just gave y'all 18 a game. At the point guard position. And you go draft a point guard?"

Steve Mills is talking all this black dude stuff with me, like we're brothers and all this. He's saying that shit, making me think it's going to make us closer. Come on, be yourself.

I loved New York. We were losing but I felt I was playing great. I felt like they still could have built something—or attempted to. They got rid of me but I definitely wanted to stay there.

It was a new way of basketball life for me, to not be sure where I was going to play next. I knew I'd be playing, so I just focused on working out, keep up with rehab, get in shape, and have to show you again.

13

I WASN'T WORRIED ABOUT NOT PLAYING AGAIN. I believed I had a chance to play somewhere, though BJ said there weren't a lot of teams calling. For me, I felt like it was just the Cavs. That really was my only way back into the league.

It really was sort of my dream team at the time. It seemed right. I knew I had to accept the minimum, even after all that talk about max contracts, because I put myself in that situation. I was the one who left New York like that.

Even going to Minnesota in summer 2018, it's because of the way I left New York; maybe there were people who didn't believe in me. It's going to hang over me until I play consistent basketball for two, three years. I think it will go away then. I put myself in that position, but that's okay because I did that for myself. I'm not worried about that. Nobody to blame but me. But I grew from the whole situation. So I felt again like it helped me become a better man. And that's worth it. Why should I have any regrets? I know I fucked up. But I got a lot out of it, a clear mind.

I was excited to play with that Cavs team, with Bron and D-Wade. To be back with a team that was going deep in the playoffs, no matter what my role would be. I had chances to go to a losing team maybe for more money, but I didn't want to go play for a losing team. I already had put in my mind that if I was going to play, I wanted to play for a contender.

When Cleveland called, I wanted to go there right away. I agreed to sign even before Kyrie got traded, so that was a surprise, too. But it was like, "I'm still going there. I don't know how my playing time is gonna be." I thought I was going there with Kyrie, but then it all changed. Hey, it worked with Bron and Kyrie, and Kyrie's also a slasher.

Being in Cleveland was cool. The whole atmosphere was different. Their equipment is different. You could tell they won a championship recently. I hadn't been around that. You could tell by their facility. The team was great, the coaching staff was great, first class.

But then it was just all downhill. I was killing in camp, in the preseason, but then I got injured and it was the same thing. My ankle this time.

That came from Greg Monroe taking me out of the air in the Milwaukee game, second game of the season. We were winning. I was playing good, had something like 12 points in about 20 minutes, six free throws, beating guys to the basket. I was playing good before that, if you were watching.

I landed flat on my left ankle and sprained it real bad. I think it was the ligament or something was messed up, and it aggravated the bone spur that was there. I couldn't run for like a month and a half.

They probably thought I was lying. Like, you know, "He just don't want to play." But I wasn't able to run. I'm thinking again, I'm done. My ankle just gave out. And nobody can explain it. There was this weird spot on my ankle and again I'm not able to do anything.

So, yeah, I left Cleveland. I thought I was done. Me and my girl left. Made sure my son was alright, got the plane tickets, didn't tell anybody. We just got the flights and went to Mexico in November.

Again, trying to figure out what's best. I can't run at all, no one is saying what's wrong. Yes, I could have retired and would have been alright with that, but I have to think about my kids. I still loved the game, don't get me wrong. Once I get in it, once I get on the floor, everything goes away. That's what's good about it, the competing. Then it doesn't matter how I felt a day ago, a year ago. None of it. It is what it is. "Okay, we're about to compete."

But with everything I'd been through, to have it happen again, an injury, and nobody is believing it, like all over again in Chicago, in New York. People were always believin' it was for the money or other stuff.

I just needed time to work things out again. I wasn't playing, but again people went crazy because I left the team.

Because of the Knicks thing. I knew Joakim went on numerous vacations with the Bulls when he wasn't playing in season. He'd come back with a tan. "You in Hawaii, bro?" I'd seen that.

I remember that one year when Bron first got back with Cleveland, he took off and went somewhere, back to Miami, I think. Gone about two weeks. But, yeah, they acted like it was a problem only with me.

I just didn't understand what went wrong. I left, of course, so that's on me. But when I came back I really tried my hardest to get on the court.

By then they had other plans. I thought I was busting my ass with them when I could play. If anything, they'd have to kick me off the court because I was doing too much. That was before the season even started. Excited, playing with a great team, a team that just went to the Finals three years in a row. Playing with a great player. Other great players. Everything was great.

It was just that I felt right away like they didn't need me. Me, I was just looking for my opportunity. Like what happened with Thibs later in Minnesota. My body finally started feeling healthy again, my knees felt good. I hadn't really even worked on my knees in a long time.

And, like I said, I was excited about playing with Bron. It was kind of weird when you look up to someone like I did with him in school and then you have the opportunity of going head-to-head against him, even though he's three, four years older. I could challenge him. But also learn from him, the way he controls the game. He paces himself throughout the game. When he was younger, he played way faster. Now he paces himself throughout the game. You up 10 in the fourth quarter, he can turn it on and win, sometimes comfortably.

When we played against each other, there were times I pushed him to a limit. Not every time, but there were times. I looked up to him as a great player. At the time people were talking like Kobe was everything, Bron was on his way up. He had stardom in him. I saw that. At the time, I was playing the three in high school, off the ball. Our games were kind of similar, where we can control the game by scoring a lot and getting a feel for the game, so I learned a lot watching him in high school.

I wasn't a basketball head, like with posters on the wall, a fanatic. I appreciated and respected people's games. It's a part of chasing greatness. I'll tell you, he deserves everything he's got right now, period. To stay consistent like that throughout every year—you know how hard that is?

Bron was cool when I was in Cleveland. But we never had an open relationship. Just teammates. Never talked about the games we played against one another. But he was cool to be around. Real professional, entertaining. He was an extrovert. It was great to be around him, because you're watching greatness every day, seeing his work ethic. I learned how much he took care of his body. Always does something in the morning, whether it's lifting, basketball recovery, whatever. He's on top of everything. Fifteen years in and he's still in that.

He controlled a lot there, but with a player like that, I mean, yeah, why not? He kind of has a right to have a say over everything given what he's done. It wasn't disrespect with any of them. I just wasn't part of his thing. I had my friends I'm cool with. I know how to be in a work environment and be peaceful. Some probably resent it, but it's where I'm from; you're trying to survive. You get beat up every day, yet you show any sign of fear, you're a pussy, and it's different. You can't. I'm not gonna kiss your ass.

That's also what hurt me with them in Cleveland in the end. I went to some dinners with those guys, but as far as going out and all that, the stuff they were doing, the dressing up, whatever, I was in my room. Isaiah Thomas and Jae Crowder were the same way. You gotta understand, with me, I had just had that court case. I was on trial. I wasn't going to be seen doing anything even if it was just being out.

When I left the Cavs, I didn't tell anybody until we were in Mexico. I didn't tell anybody because I felt even though me and my family talked the first time, they didn't really hear me. I was okay to go back to New York after I left there, and I understood what I had to do, but I didn't have it fully worked out in Cleveland, not after being hurt again. They didn't understand where I was coming from. So, I did feel like I had to leave. If I would have mentioned it to anybody or said what it was, my family would have tried to stop it again.

I went down to Mexico and did a lot of thinking, a lot of praying, a lot of writing. I've always kept a journal. No one's ever seen it. Whenever I write, it's always giving thanks to whoever's watching me.

Whenever I'm writing in my journal, it's always as if I'm having a conversation with that person. It's a way for me to feel like I'm communicating my thoughts, how I'm feeling. Always giving them thanks and telling them how blessed I am for everything, asking them to forgive me for my sins—even the ones I don't notice.

I was in Mexico for a week and then came back. People say I was depressed, but I feel too blessed to be depressed about anything. Don't get me wrong. I know depression is real. My Cavs teammate Kevin Love talked about that. I know people go through that and it's tough and they can't control it. They say you're rich or famous so things are good and will go away. No. I just needed time to figure out and organize myself and figure out a path or a way to make this transition as smooth as possible, including knowing what I was going to do after basketball. There were a lot of people thinking basketball was over for me. I had to work through that.

I PLAY VIDEO GAMES WHEN WE TRAVEL. I read sometimes.

But mostly I play chess.

I'm a big chess player and it helped me get through a lot of things because it makes you think. I play a lot online where people don't know it's me they're playing with. I'm an alright player.

When I came back with Cleveland they made me talk to a therapist because they thought I was crazy. You could tell they were thinking, "We ain't gonna put you on the court until we find out you're not having a breakdown." So when I came back I was talking to their therapist and I tell him I like to play chess and he thought I was bullshitting. So next appointment he brings a chessboard. Says I should show him. Wanted me to prove it, I guess. I kicked his ass! He was so surprised. I called my friends after that and I was like, "I kicked that therapist's ass!"

Playing chess has been one of the most important things in my life. Really. It started when I was in seventh grade. That's when I transferred schools and went to Beasley, because Randolph only went up to sixth grade. Beasley was kindergarten to eighth grade, but I only went there seventh and eighth. That was my first time seeing a chess team or even hearing about chess. It was in the lunch room and I used to just sit and watch other people play. Never said anything or played. I didn't really talk to people like that. I used to watch just to see how it was played, kind of got hooked on it right from there.

The thing was that it was just so complex. It's simple because everybody can play chess. But I also feel like it challenges you, requires patience, makes you think about what you are doing and why. Lots of quiet and long pauses. I relate it to my life, like where I lost my queen early. Right? Trouble. Now the game is being played and Derrick, he's got one of his pawns left. But he's about to take it all the way to the end to trade it in for another queen.

That's how I feel about where I'm at in my life. I lost my queen with my injuries and everything that happened. I'm battling my ass off now. There's only three pieces on the board. Your three against my three. My pawns, one of them is loose to get another queen, giving me hope. It can be like your life. That's the appeal, why chess is chess. They call it the game of life. You've got to solve problems. You're not gonna have a perfect game every game—impossible when you've got so many moves. So, figure it out. And that's why I love it.

I play solitary chess all the time. If I'm on the plane by myself, I've got it on my phone. Basically always have a chessboard with me. Chess changed my life—no bullshit. Helped me understand the strategies.

So, I saw their therapist, but I could tell the Cavs didn't really want me back. You could see that. Didn't even want me to play good so it wouldn't look bad when they got rid of me. I had a good game when we beat Indiana, with like 14 points in 15 minutes. Next game, they play me eight minutes. Then a DNP and then five minutes.

When I chose to sign with the Cavs, it's because I didn't want to sign to a team where I'm going right to vet mode and I'm on a losing team. I wanted to go to a contending team. I also wanted to go somewhere that had premier players, like playing with a Bron.

I remember when I was signing there with the new GM, Koby Altman. We had dinner. He was acting so excited, telling me, "I can't believe my first signing is D-Rose." Nobody is telling him to say that. We're eating and he just randomly says that.

Okay, I can respect that, cool. But then it's the same guy who sends me to Utah.

If you really were excited, really wanted me, you would at least hear me out with what I'm going through, keep me the rest of the year. I know I could have helped that team. You didn't have to trade me if you really cared. "Okay, I'm gonna leave him around this year to watch him. Maybe next year we think of getting rid of him. But at least for this year we got you." Then I'm traded to Utah a couple weeks after that. People looking out for themselves. You have to see that.

I didn't have to deal with that when I first came in to the NBA because back then my talent trumped all that. But everyone who goes to a job learns that eventually. They always love the new guys.

I didn't have to deal with or really understand the league at first. Then people are saying to you, "Bro, why aren't you bringing in anybody with you? You supposed to have some help!" That's how the league is going, people getting help.

I'm walking on the street, random people come up to me, "Y'all getting somebody else? Y'all play too many minutes, bro." That was stuff I didn't know. You look at so many people in the league, MJ, Magic, I'm thinking I'm doing my thing like they did. Looking back now, it's like, "Damn, it would have been a little easier if I had a little help." But it wasn't something you were thinking about so much.

I was just about to have my baby girl and I was in Cleveland working out after they traded me and then I was released by Utah. Just going to Cleveland State with my friend Art, working out. I didn't know what was going on in Cleveland, but you could see. They knew they were gonna get rid of me. When I had the quick 14 against Indiana I could tell they didn't want that to happen. So they sat me on the bench the last couple of games after that and then I was traded.

I DIDN'T KNOW WHAT WOULD BE NEXT after I got released by Utah, but I didn't think my career was over. I was surprised to end up back with Thibs, Taj, Jimmy, with all of them, in Minnesota. But I can say it gave me time to really appreciate everything I went through prior to getting there, because when I got there, I don't know, but it just felt like I was finally home.

Going to New York never did feel right. Going to Cleveland, I'm there and I'm trying, but also it just didn't feel right. With Minnesota, Thibs was honest. Even when he didn't play me when I first got there, he was just telling me the politics of it. "They have certain people here, they feel like they need to play certain people." He was just telling me to stick with him. I stuck with him and he looked out for me. That's one of the reasons I wanted to come back.

And then there was Jimmy.

The funny part about what was going on between Thibs and Minnesota management was, in Chicago me and Jimmy were supposed to be the ones having problems. We weren't close, but there were never problems. And like I said, in Minnesota, when all that trade stuff came up, he came to me to talk about some of the stuff going on. We were texting back and forth when all the crazy media stuff was going on because, yeah, I know something about that.

But I also had to play the veteran role with the young guys. I wasn't going to play a part in it with the media. I told Jimmy my perspective on it, but my big message to him was not to lose your leverage. Oscar and those guys fought too hard for what we have to handle it wrong and hand the leverage back to the team.

That was also good for my relationship with the young guys. They saw I handled it the same way with everyone, with love and respect, so they came to me for advice. I feel like they liked my presence on the team. But I also could understand what Jimmy was feeling.

Look, it wasn't his fault. It's the league's fault. Nothing against Karl-Anthony Towns, he's cool—and he's good. But you get these kids and you spoil them before they achieve something. Get their first contracts at $190 million. Come on. Now you got a situation where a young player can voice his opinion to fire a coach or get anybody on that staff fired if he doesn't like what's going on. That's a lot of power. What, 21, 22 years old? No guidance, but money and power. And he wasn't guided into it, but thrust. I know things change, but that's not even the way it was when I came in the league—and it shouldn't be.

I had to play to make myself the number one pick. You don't gotta do shit in the tournament now for that. I felt I had to prove myself. It was still a debate with me and Beasley going number one right up to almost draft day. Kids now, you don't even gotta make it to the tournament. Markelle Fultz? Ben Simmons? Good players, but you can't even get your team to the tournament?

But the league is like, "Oh, we can already tell he's gonna be good. He's gonna be max." You can see it. But at the same time, who is giving this kid guidance? Is it enough? Is it good? That's how I feel about it—and Jimmy, too. So now you have all these kids where they feel like they're super entitled, and what did they do? That's what we got right now. It's a big problem for the league.

Jimmy was feeling, "Why'd y'all pay them first when I was the one that got you to the playoffs?" That's all it was. Jimmy wasn't doing it right, though he was right. So we talked. I'd tell him that you gotta be able to control yourself a lot better; you're inside a billionaires club. These guys talk every day. They know everything. So why give them that leverage by staying away from the team? Just making it hard on yourself.

Yeah, I think Jimmy was surprised when I reached out to him like that. Probably fucking surprised. Jimmy's a good dude. Just wanted what's right.

And then all that crazy stuff about how he went to practice and showed up everyone? It's the new league, man. He came in and he played hard, period. Scored one time in that practice they were all writing about. Yes, one basket. Right hand up to God. What's so exciting about that? But the media is going crazy. You would think he scored 30. That's why I don't feed into this shit anymore.

It was killing Thibs, I'll tell you. He wasn't saying anything to us, but you could tell he was taking it hard. Jimmy was a big piece for us, and in the West, of course, we knew we needed him. But we were feeling to start the season like we'd be alright. KAT, Andrew Wiggins, guys are just young. They bring the intensity and I felt we'd be really good. So my role was becoming to watch everybody closely. Right, me.

I felt like me being this vet, my job was to make everybody feel at ease on the team, communicating, talking way more than I ever did before. But now I'm 30, 10 years in the league. It's the most talking I ever did.

For me, just trying to keep growing, do the right thing for my teammates, but not with the assists on the court now—maybe assists in other ways. Those texts are something I damn sure wouldn't have sent Jimmy a few years ago. Trying just to give him perspective from things I've been through. Like, "I've been there, bro. The way you're handling it right now, you're gonna give them that leverage to say fuck you. And they're gonna stand on you just like they trying to stand on me."

I wouldn't suggest anyone do what I did. Especially if they weren't financially alright. I was seeing him heading down that road, so I felt I had to reach out. "You already got one knee surgery. You're 29, 30. They shit on you—shit on you very quickly."

Jimmy got a good trade out of it. I hope it works out for him.

But it doesn't for a lot of guys. Look at Isaiah Thomas. What he's going through. Still wasn't playing halfway into the 2018 season. After all he did for Boston and still hasn't gotten right—run out of Cleveland. That's what I mean. "Don't let them shit on you. Don't give them that leverage." Right now we as players, we have that leverage. I told Jimmy, "You got the talent, you got the leverage—all the leverage in the world." I told Jimmy I understand the way he brings intensity to practice. I played with Joakim, Kurt Thomas. I know what kind of assholes they were every day. Just talk shit all day. I'm with that. But at the same time, you've got to be smarter.

Jimmy was still too angry to listen until the trade. I told him he needed to play chess. Chess gets you to think a couple moves ahead. Not act emotionally. Maybe chess can save his life, too.

ALL THE STUFF WITH JIMMY was overshadowing everything to start the season, but I was excited, feeling really good. I was even making threes when the season started. I felt like

I finally got my balance back. I feel like that 2018 summer I did everything right. I lifted but I didn't lift too much. I did a lot of basketball workouts, more than the last three or four summers. Getting strong without overcompensating for my legs. I was missing my rhythm at hooping. I wasn't playing as much. So that summer I reverted back to playing as much as possible. Every year, I look forward to the games, but this felt really good. Probably best I felt about basketball since my last year with the Bulls, maybe right before I got smashed in the eye.

I really did feel like, going into the 2018 season, I was going to be making some noise again. Dead serious, man. I was where I was, just looking for an opportunity to make one more grind. It'll be the last grind and then I'll be able to do whatever I want after this. So, I got to give it my all one more time and then walk away gracefully. I can see the end now, because I want it to be that way and not because it *has* to be that way. That's what I was thinking in the summer before the season.

I want to play a few more years. It's crazy to think I'm already at 10 years with everything that's happened—way more than most guys get to play. I've been blessed. It feels right again. If the biggest problem in Minnesota is dealing with kids, I'm cool with that. That's something that's fixable: "Grow the fuck up." Call them on their shit every time. No problem. I'll take that over all the other bullshit. That's what I'm trying to tell them. "The situation y'all are in right now?

Cherish it. Because you can go somewhere and the shit can be all different, where you're mad and the GM is on your ass—or maybe the owner. Just be grateful that you can handle this situation."

Then there was the 50-point game. Halloween night. A lot of crazy things about that night, but I really did feel like it was meant to happen. Like, out of all the bullshit I went through, all the adversity I went through, it was my way of showing myself that I still have it. If I put it all together, it would be what that game looked like.

That 50 points was my "I'll show you." I knew I still had it in me. I always believed that, but I know hardly anyone did. Maybe my friends and family—and Thibs.

But it was the way that game went that I feel showed and meant the most to me. It was having a game like that—and winning. A lot of people overlooked that I had a blocked shot on Dante Exum at the end—up by three with three seconds left—to seal the game. That's what I care about. Fifty is one thing, but if you lose, who cares? Thirty and lose, so what? But to have 50—and I also missed three free throws, so I could have had 50-something points—and seal it with two free throws with about 13 seconds left and then to get a block, that's really why all the emotions came out afterward.

Remember, they were leading with just over a minute left. No matter how many points I'm scoring, if we don't win that game, what does it matter?

With us being shorthanded and Thibs and the team rely-
ing on me, it meant so much. Not so much that it was like
it used to be, but that I still could do it after everything I'd
been through. I was emotional because of me always believing. I told people I'd come back and get a max again, not
sayin' it for the money, but for what it meant—a max means
you're there again.

I know it's crazy that I've always had this belief in myself,
that I didn't care what anybody thought about me. Sure, I
cared what was said sometimes because of how it affected the
people who mean the most to me, which is something people
don't think about when things are written or said. But a few
people know how much work I put into my craft, and those
are my best friends, and that's what's important to me. We
talk about it all the time, having a game like that. But then
to actually go out and have the opportunity to do it and to
get up 30 reps in a game? When was the last time I'd shot
30 times in a game?

You got certain guys who do that on a nightly basis now
the way things are. Not to call out anyone, but the young
boy from Utah shot 35 times in one game about the same
time. Nothing unusual, though. Guys do that on a regular
basis now. I've talked about that before. You don't get the
reps, you aren't going to be doing the things you did before.
Healthy or whatever. So then what happens if one game I
get my reps up like that?

But the only reason I did that was we were down players. Jimmy didn't play. Jeff Teague, Tyus Jones, all out. I'm never looking to do that. I've always been about my teammates unless I had to score. I felt I had to take on that load before the game. I wasn't thinking 50, of course, but I felt I had to do some things I don't usually try to do.

I know how hard I work and I know I'm talented. Sometimes people try to discourage you when they know you're talented, to talk crap about you and hope you quit, give up. I remember playing dice games where you know someone's got the hot hand on the dice and you talk shit to them because you know they're good. Maybe they won't finish it.

I'm not in Minnesota looking back after a game like that and laughing or holding any grudges or thinking, "I told you so," like with the Knicks. I could have held a grudge the way it ended, but that was the old me, the young, dumb me. Thibs and the Minnesota team, they were allowing me to play the way I normally play, and the way that I'm playing today is way more controlled and efficient than how I played in the past.

So rather than hold a grudge, I look at my time in New York as a blessing in disguise. It allowed me to learn how to be the third option playing with Porzingis and Melo, figure out how to affect the game in my own way. I played in the triangle and I still got my average, 18 per game in the triangle being a third option. Doesn't that say something? The old me, I would have been pissed off at the GM and feeling down about everybody there. But I learned something there.

I learned how to float through a game and still affect it in my own way. That's a big thing. It's maturity and time, growing up, trying to figure out who I am as a man.

Yes, I know I'm very stubborn. I'm not going to lean on anyone to teach me something. I feel like I can figure everything out myself, and going through that process with the injuries, with New York and then Cleveland, made me more vulnerable in a way. To my family, I'm the breadwinner. I understand that. It's like no one wants to see the guy who is making everything happen being down or looking and feeling vulnerable.

So, you always have to have on that exterior or put up that wall, like you have to be strong for everybody else. But when they saw I was opening up, when I showed what I showed, it's when everything changed. Like my former teammate Kevin Love would say, "Live your truth, say what you have to say, and don't be afraid."

It's a blessing to see, because I know what every player is going through. In a way, all of us in the league are stubborn and proud—you have to work to get to the league. From the outside, it's all glamour, but inside it's the grind. And we're all people going through the same feelings. It don't matter how much is in your bank account. It doesn't mean you can't feel a certain way.

Things are going to change for every player, just like you at your job. You may be hot now, but you also know when you get to a certain age or certain position, things change.

There's only a few LeBrons ever who can be hot when they enter the league and all the way to year 15 still hot the same way. You saw it with Melo, the way they were saying, "Your story is over, we don't want to hear your story no more. We done with you. Hey, let's see this next kid, Giannis, who everyone is talking about." You knew then it would happen to him, too. Just living.

But with all of that, it doesn't mean they stop talking about you, that your story is done. That's really how I always felt. You decide your story, no matter what they say. I know what type of talent I have, and you say that and people think you're lying to yourself or you're crazy. But I did feel I just needed the opportunity, and I came to Minnesota and I'm part of a franchise where the coach believed in me.

All these other places, they say they believe in you, and then you're running the triangle offense. "Okay, you don't believe in me. If you believed in me, you would have changed the offense. Cleveland, you say you believe in me and by the end of the year I am getting DNPs. Ty Lue, I like you, nothing against you, but you don't know how good I am."

Then I go to Minnesota with Thibs and, if anything, he's watching my health from Day 1. I'm not doing too much and I think it's because we've been around each other for a long time and we can talk to each other and we can communicate. That's big for coaches. It's something I read wrong with some of the other coaches, not having that communication me and Thibs have.

The funny part is a lot of people don't understand our connection. They say, "He's the one who got you injured!" What! Thibs wasn't telling me what to think when I was out there. And not to sound crazy, but I believe in spiritual things. At that time I was too hot. I came out of nowhere, I was adding a lot of pressure to the league, and you never know what people wish on you. Not saying stuff happens because people want it to, but I do believe in karma, good and bad. And there are evil thoughts. I felt I wasn't protected that much and now I really feel like I am protected.

There's this communication I have with Thibs that's different. Jeff's hurt, so I'll say to him, "Let Tyus start."

He'll say, "No, you're starting!"

Okay, cool, but we will talk it out, say what we want and think. Then just play. I'm not trying to step on anybody's toes because I know I'm in Minnesota to adhere to that veteran role, just be part of the team, chill, just no pressure.

You don't realize it until you get older, but even as a kid it's pressure when you come up like I did. I've been having pressure since I've been in fifth, sixth grade, playing in Chicago. Not just the big games like everyone has, but being compared, being the next one. Then you get to the league and it's just more of it.

I remember so many nights I couldn't sleep because I was worrying about the game. Not about who I'm playing, but just the game. I want to perform—they need me to perform. It really used to drive me crazy. I felt that pressure to perform and even though I knew I put in the work, you want to go out and get the results. I know it's a game and everyone wants to play games, but who goes to work and it's in front of all these people and everyone is telling you "Good game," "You're shit," this and that?

Now, it's none of that. Not that I don't feel it's as important, but now I just go out and see what the game needs. Not forcing shots, but gauging the game. Coming off the bench? No problem. That's why I said before the 2018 season I could win Sixth Man of the Year.

Yeah, years ago I was saying MVP before the season and now I'm saying Sixth Man. But that is the right approach, I think. I have to put my pride to the side and understand at this stage of my career what's important.

I could be this mad dude, mad I'm not starting. But then I think, "What if my son sees that and hears about that later on and he tries to use that as an excuse someday, act spoiled in the corporate world, just expecting to get what he wants because of who he is?"

No, you grind your way to a promotion, to the top. Don't expect it, work for it. None of this was handed to me. I had to work to be the top pick. I'm chasing O.J. Mayo the whole time through high school and then get to be the first pick. Then I'm coming to the league and even with the Bulls I knew the debate was me or Michael Beasley. Michael was great at the time and if you want him, cool. I get it. So even with everything that happened, I always felt I had to prove myself. I felt I had to do that the whole time I was in the league, no matter what was happening. That's why it came out the way it did, with me and the MVP: "Why can't I win it?"

You know how it was then: "Get the fuck out of here."

Look, you asked me the question. Why are you asking me the question if you don't want my answer?

So even now, alright, y'all wrote me off. A lot were saying I should retire not knowing what I was going through, ex-players acting like they've never been in my shoes before. You know, "He's done, he'll average six or eight points. Get rid of him." But the way I look at it is, I feel every great act reinvents themselves at some point, and that's what I did.

It's not just being a student of the game. I talked with Thibs about Tim Hardaway, the way he played in Golden State and then getting hurt, moved on, and coming back in Miami to be an All-Star and a leader. I look at the big acts, like a Frank Sinatra, the way he was on top as a pop singer and actor and then it's over for him and then he comes back with the big bands and ballads and a different style. He started in one environment and switched all the way up. I look at a guy like Robert Downey Jr., a star actor and then he has drug problems and is even in prison and comes back to be one of the biggest stars ever. Come on, everything he went through? He could have given up and his story would have been over. But it's how he took everything in and used it as part of his change. At some point you have to be vulnerable and understand and accept what's happened and know who you are and what you can do and don't let others write your ending.

Sometimes I even think that getting that championship I wanted so much in those early years might have made it all even crazier down the road. Maybe whoever is watching over me did all that for a reason, my injuries and all that, so I could see everything for what it is, see people for who they really are, who really is in my corner, who jumped off the boat when it was on fire.

Now I feel like we're riding. I know my friends, my family, who has my back, and you can't buy that or just ask for it. It takes hardship and tough times to get there—so much shit sometimes—and maybe a championship would have been too much for me at the time. You don't know.

MY STORY IS BIGGER THAN ME. They can't control what's going to happen. You don't know what will happen with my story. I know it will be something good, though, by the way I'm giving, the way I'm treating people—my mom, my family, everyone—and how I have my principles in order.

I'm following my guidelines to my life, listening to my omens, reading my signs. Everyone has them in their lives, the things that matter to you. I always knew how hard I was working, no matter what was being said, and it came out on the floor in Minnesota, how I want to be and how I want to play. I got there by finding my comfort zone on the team and learning my role.

Yes, it was me who fucked up in the past with the decisions I made. No one else. I'm man enough to say that and know at the time I needed help. Look, in Cleveland I didn't know I was going to be taken out of the air and wouldn't be able to run for a month. It just happened. I left Cleveland—my choice, my decision.

But I don't feel like this is the last chapter in my life. I feel like I have a lot more to add to society, and being the person I am and the heart I have, I feel I can do a lot more for my people. Because it's knowing my past that got me here. So I can't forget friends, fans, family, the past, loved ones telling me the truth, being mindful of that all the time. You keep fighting because you never know who's looking.

The biggest thing for me still, though, even with all that, is winning.

It's like at first I was trying to get my money, financially be good, like every player does. I was just being honest and so I said it. But especially now, after going through everything, it's like I want to show people I can hoop and help the young guys along the way. I had a chance to see and experience the ups and downs. So why not share that?

Shit, I'm the MVP and then practically kicked out of the league. Basically getting cut and practicing at Cleveland State, trying to find a team. Oklahoma City was talking about picking me up that season when I was back at Cleveland State working out on my own. But then Thibs reached out and asked me to just wait, to take my time. I was ready. I was ready to show everyone again.

I feel it progressed in the right way. I feel like I can adapt. That was one of the reasons I want to continue to play. I want you to look up and not pay attention to what I'm doing and it will be 15 years in, and it's like, "Damn, you're still in!" I want that. I feel like I've still got a lot left. So right now I'm just looking for the opportunity. I feel once I get the opportunity, if I get any look at it, I'm taking advantage of it.

I don't worry about being hurt. The last time I thought about being hurt was probably my second injury. After that, I didn't think about it. It was tiresome. Just having faith, knowing this is out of my control. Only thing I can do is put myself in the position to succeed. I love all that right now, where my mind is at. I'm enjoying all that right now more than anything. When I was younger and so caught up in chasing or being great, trying to get these accolades, I wasn't fucking enjoying it. Not like now.

Now I'm showing it.

Timeline

Derrick Martell Rose

October 4, 1988: Born, Chicago, IL

March 18, 2006: Leads Simeon to Illinois state high school basketball championship with winning shot against Peoria Richwoods in overtime

March 31, 2007: Selected Illinois Mr. Basketball

April 7, 2008: Leads Memphis to NCAA tournament championship game, loses to Kansas in overtime

June 26, 2008: Selected first overall in the NBA draft by the Chicago Bulls

October 28, 2008: Makes NBA debut for Bulls with 11 points and nine assists

April 18, 2009: Matches Kareem Abdul-Jabbar's rookie playoff scoring record with 36 points to beat the defending champion Boston Celtics in Game 1

April 22, 2009: Named NBA Rookie of the Year

January 28, 2010: Named to the NBA's Eastern Conference All-Stars, the first Bull to be selected since Michael Jordan in 1998

May 3, 2011: Becomes youngest Most Valuable Player in NBA history in almost unanimous vote

December 21, 2011: Signs maximum contract extension through 2016–17 with Bulls

December 25, 2011: Opens lockout-shortened season with game-winning shot to defeat the Los Angeles Lakers

April 28, 2012: Tears anterior cruciate ligament in left knee with 1:20 remaining and Bulls leading by 12 points in Game 1 of playoffs against Philadelphia 76ers

May 12, 2012: Undergoes surgery at Rush University Medical Center, where surgeon Brian Cole estimates a return no sooner than 12 months later

November 22, 2013: Suffers torn meniscus in right knee in 10th game back following ACL surgery, misses rest of season after surgery on November 25, 2013

September 14, 2014: Leads Team USA with six assists in gold medal game win over Serbia in FIBA World Cup

February 23, 2015: Tears meniscus in right knee after 46 games

April 8, 2015: Returns with nine points in 19 minutes

April 18, 2015: Scores 23 points in first playoff game since ACL tear and averages 21.5 points in series win over Milwaukee Bucks

May 8, 2015: Scores 30 points, including game-winning three-pointer as Bulls take 2–1 lead over Cleveland in Eastern Conference semifinals; Cavs win next three games

September 29, 2015: Suffers orbital fracture in first practice of season

June 22, 2016: Traded to New York Knicks, along with Justin Holiday, for Jerian Grant, Jose Calderon, and Robin Lopez

January 9, 2017: Leaves team to return home for one day and misses game against New Orleans Pelicans

April 2, 2017: Tears meniscus in left knee and misses rest of season after averaging 18 points in 64 games

July 25, 2017: Signs with Cavaliers

November 24, 2017: Leaves team for personal reasons after playing in seven games

January 18, 2018: Scores nine points in 13 minutes in return to Cavaliers

February 8, 2018: Traded to Utah Jazz; waived February 10

March 8, 2018: Signs with Minnesota Timberwolves

July 4, 2018: Re-signs with Timberwolves

October 31, 2018: Scores career-high 50 points in win over Jazz